# THE MAKING OF
# GUYS AND DOLLS

## Keith Garebian

mosaic press

National Library of Canada Cataloguing in Publication Data

Garebian, Keith, 1943-
    The making of Guys and dolls

Includes bibliographical references.
ISBN 0-88962-764-9

    1. Loesser, Frank, 1910-1969. Guys and dolls. I. Title.

ML410.L796G22 2002            782.1'4            C 2002-903812-7

Published by Mosaic Press, offices and warehouse at 1252 Speers Road, Units 1 and 2, Oakville, Ontario, L6L 5N9, Canada and Mosaic Press, PMB 145, 4500 Witmer Industrial Estates, Niagara Falls, NY, 14305-1386, U.S.A.

Mosaic Press acknowledges the assistance of the Canada Council and the Department of Canadian Heritage, Government of Canada for their support of our publishing programme.

Mosaic Press in Canada:
1252 Speers Road, Units 1 & 2,
Oakville, Ontario
L6L 5N9
Phone/Fax: 905-825-2130
mosaicpress@on.aibn.com

Mosaic Press in U.S.A.:
4500 Witmer Industrial Estates
PMB 145, Niagara Falls, NY
14305-1386
Phone/Fax: 1-800-387-8992
mosaicpress@on.aibn.com

Le Conseil des Arts    The Canada Council
du Canada    for the Arts

FOR LEON AND MARIA MARTIN

# TABLE OF CONTENTS

# GOLDEN MUSICAL

**GUYS AND DOLLS** opened at the forty-sixth theatre in 1950 as (what Gerald Bordman calls) "a tough-talking, bighearted musicalization of Damon Runyon's sagas of New York low life." Though certainly not something to make you think of Wilde or Coward or even Neil Simon, *Guys and Dolls* is a triumph of the comic spirit, dependent on Broadway for color, yet enlarged beyond a merely local significance. Lindy's (where a mug can certainly bet a small bundle on the ratio of cheesecake to strudel), the Hot Box Night Club (where a showgirl can develop a cold from, among other things, her scant clothing), the sidewalks bursting with shady characters, the labyrinthine sewers where pin-striped crapshooters race into action, and the neon-splashed skyline can't be anywhere but New York. But then there's that romantic, tipsy, moonlit interlude in Havana with Sky and his "Mission doll" that is quite beyond the Manhattan grain. Yet, there is something undeniably American about this musical that is captured in its racy argot, breezy manner, high, raucous energy, and eager willingness to gamble on enterprises that could bring in the cops.

Virtually everything about the show is now legend—right from the Jo Swerling-Abe Burrows libretto, the irrepressible Frank Loesser score, and the bright, stylized sets of Jo Mielziner to the rousing choreography by Michael Kidd, the costumes of Alvin Colt, and the performances of Sam Levene, Robert Alda, Vivian Blaine, Stubby Kaye, and B.S. Pully. The whole show was phenomenal, and almost everybody who saw the original production was convinced that it was musical comedy at its absolute peak.

There were, of course, some high-minded critics who complained about the subject matter, characters, and milieu. But even the most cerebral drama critics who usually sneered at Broadway musicals as if they were manifestations of cultural genocide were charmed by the show. No less an eminence than Eric Bentley, the most uncompromising of this breed, was moved to declare that Guys and Dolls was "possibly the best of all American musical comedies," and that such musical comedy was "the most lively part of the American theatre" of the day. Bentley was not being whimsical or indulging in a passing fancy. He included the libretto in his anthology, From the American Drama (1956), thereby shocking the literati by omitting O'Neill, Miller, and Williams, but later defending his choice in a 1964 talk, "Comedy and the Comic Spirit in America" by arguing that this musical, unlike most serious American plays, was not a second-rate European imitation but one that "draws upon the rhythm of American life—or, to be more precise, upon certain rhythms in American life—in order to create living theatre." Allowing that the work is superficial ("If indeed it were ever not superficial, it would tumble into bathos"), that it "has little or no value as a document," and that "as a naturalistic study of milieu it is non-existent," Bentley was deeply struck by its comic quality which he called "inalienably American."

It took producers of rare vision to conceive of Damon Runyon's stories as material for a musical, especially as the characters in them spoke in a specially invented and racy argot that, although well known to and enjoyed by Runyon's numerous newspaper and magazine readers, was virtually a foreign language to the musical stage. As a critic noted, the style "distort[ed] and diminish[ed] the value of the speech patterns of the respectable middle-class society that [Runyon] satirized." Moreover, the real charm and skill of the stories lay in the narrator's personality and technique, and the narrator's role was certain to vanish in the Broadway musical. Then, too, even if some of the stories could be combined and modified for the stage, what would the dominant element be? Picaresque comedy? Satire? Romance?

Could a Broadway musical become a success without romance? Virtually every musical was a love story, and the temper of the era demanded light entertainment. *Kiss Me, Kate* had made its début a mere two years earlier, and although the plot and subplot in it were cleverly integrated with beautiful support from Cole Porter's music, Hanya Holm's choreography, and Lemuel Ayres' stylized sets, this was still basically semi-operetta material, modulated by Sam and Bella Spewack (with Shakespeare's inveterate assistance) into clever satire. Audiences didn't feel the characters were much of a gamble: after all, the feuding pair who find themselves cast as Kate and Petruchio in a revival of *The Taming of the Shrew* had wonderfully robust literary antecedents and inspiration. Then, too, the classic battle of the sexes lent itself naturally to rousing high comedy with, of course, calculated possibilities of rekindled romance for the co-stars who were once married to each other.

But *Guys and Dolls* was a risk. Its principals were notorious gamblers and their "dolls." And the supporting cast, "nice old-fashioned delinquents" (Bentley's phrase), was drawn chiefly from a sleazy netherworld, though the characters had colourful nicknames that promised many a laugh for the monikers themselves. What's in a name? In Runyon's stories, the names were often emblems of the characters: Nicely-Nicely Jones, Harry The Horse, Big Jule, Sky Masterson, Rusty Charlie, Big Nig Skolsky, Angie the Ox, Sam the Gonoph, Good Time Charley, Rochester Red, Dave the Dude, Feet Samuels, Brandy Bottle Bates, Miss Midgie Muldoon, Handsome Jack, Miss Missouri Martin, the Lemon Drop Kid.

The names were deliciously comic but how would they serve the romance? And the fact that the libretto was to be created chiefly from "The Idyll of Miss Sarah Brown" (where a Salvation Army lass is the chief romantic figure) raised scepticism about the eventual box-office returns. After all, Sky Masterson, a compulsive gambler, wins the heart of this mission "doll" after tricking her into an exotic rendezvous in Cuba. How convincing could this be in a musical where puritanism had to rub shoulders against Manhattan sleaze? Certainly, there was potential for satire, but as George S. Kaufman, who directed the show, once cracked: "Satire is what closes Saturday night."

Everybody now knows that Abe Burrows proved the doubters wrong, despite the fact that it was his first Broadway show and he was inheriting a challenge that had hitherto defeated all-comers. His radio experience was an asset, as was the fact that he had Kaufman as the show's director. But, perhaps, the underlying reason for his success was his way of being funny and truthful, or, as he put it in a round-table Dramatists Guild symposium on comedy: "When you write it funny, you write it from the gut."

Then there were the music and lyrics—both by Frank Loesser, for whom this was only his second Broadway show. Actually, Loesser's songs were written first, and Abe Burrows had to create a story to fit them. Later, the critics spoke of the show as a great "integrated" work, but the truth of the matter was that the libretto was composed in a reversal of the usual Broadway musical order of things.

Loesser's score set a standard that many composers strove to meet. Fred Ebb, no slouch as a lyricist himself but whose musical style is far from Loesser's, wishes he'd written *Guys and Dolls* and confesses: "I wore the record of *Guys and Dolls* right down to the wire. It was the first time I'd ever done that. I just played it over and over. Not a day of my life went by that I didn't." His enthusiasm is matched by that of other lyricists, composers, and librettists. Years after the Broadway premiere, when many of these were asked to name their favourite Broadway lyricist, the name of Frank Loesser was warmly mentioned in the company of Oscar Hammerstein II, Alan Jay Lerner, Cole Porter, Lorenz Hart, Harold Arlen, Ira Gershwin, Irving Berlin, E.Y. Harburg, Howard Dietz, and a few others. Matt Dubey, lyricist of Happy Hunting, selected "Adelaide's Lament" as a song that made his life happier in the musical theatre. Screen lyricist Norman Gimbel cited the same number for its "perception, originality, technique and production value," while Morrie Ryskind, librettist of Strike Up The Band and co-author of Animal Crackers and Of Thee, I Sing, picked the entire score because "it was so integrated into the book that it was hard to tell where the dialogue left off and the music began."

Burrows and Loesser understood the importance of each other's work, but though he guided the show to its ultimate perfection, director George S. Kaufman seemed to barely tolerate the score. A perfectionist to his finger-tips, Kaufman was impatient about the musical end of things.

Yet the show worked marvellously well. The material was so superbly crafted that the seams were invisible, and Guys and Dolls fairly glittered with its utter lack of pretension. It was raffish and very funny; it was humorously sentimental; it was romantic and naughty too; and it was truthful in its own mischievous manner.

The show became a box-office sensation, and even Abe Burrows claimed to have trouble getting tickets to see it again. In July 1951, he mused about its success for Theatre Arts, stating categorically that it was a hit not because of individual performers who carried it on their shoulders, not because of a great score alone, and certainly not because of a great moment or two—such as a ballet or a novel production number. Guys and Dolls was a hit because "everything fits. Everything goes together." Expanding on this idea, he wrote: "Nothing is there that doesn't belong. There are no love ballads which are written in a different language from the dialogue. When a mug sings a love-song it's a mug-type love-song. The dances are strictly in character. There's a crap game ballet which looks like a crap game. A real Runyon crap game." In this show, he revealed, the collaborators didn't care about how a single number or scene would fare in itself. They didn't care about reprising songs "for no reason at all." They cared about "the whole show and nothing went in unless it fit."

Audiences who saw it left the theatre feeling ecstatic. And they couldn't point to just one aspect of the show. It was all of a piece and it was all good. *Guys and Dolls* showed that there could really be a Golden Age of musical comedy, especially when a show had swing, style, and pizzazz.

# DAMON RUNYON
# OF BROADWAY

**CY FEUER**, a stocky man, five feet five inches tall, with brushcut grey hair and horn-rimmed glasses, was a musician who once played trumpet in the Radio City Hall orchestra. He had gone on to become musical director at Republic Pictures (1938-42; 1945-7), responsible chiefly for scoring westerns and "quickie" musicals. Ernest Martin, eight years younger and a six footer who spoke as rapidly as an auctioneer, was the son of a California lawyer and had gone to UCLA to study drama—"only because they didn't require much plugging." But even before graduation, he was working for Columbia Broadcasting in Los Angeles, first as a page, later as a writer, and eventually as a $25,000 a year producer. The two met in Hollywood where, after mulling over things, they decided to be their own bosses.

The pair had struck it rich in 1948 with *Where's Charley?*, which starred Ray Bolger in a musical comedy adaptation of the English *Charley's Aunt*. Frank Loesser had done the score which was "old-fashioned and innovative at the same time" (as Loesser's daughter put it in her memoir of him). Romantic ballads, a waltz, a traditional school song, a march, and novelty songs combined with the farcical plot, but it took the concerted efforts of George Abbott, expert director, and Ray Bolger, a star who guaranteed advance sales, to make the show work. The Phildadelphia tryout had been shaky. Loesser's first wife described the road experience as "a hornet's nest of feuds, illicit love affairs, unrehearsed ballets, unfinished orchestrations, and an overall fury at Feuer and Martin" who, because this was their first show, were determined to take it to Broadway as economically as possible. Everything seemed wrong at that stage. George Balanchine, the choreographer, had no classical ballet dancers so his ballet, "The Red Rose Cotillion," was messy and looked like a parody. The producers carrying niggardliness to extremes, had supplied the most artificial red roses ever crafted, which upset Loesser no end and which prompted Balanchine's early departure for New York where he could devote his efforts to his first love—real ballet.

Ray Bolger saved the show—but only by accident. His softshoe routine, "Once In Love with Amy," performed as a "down-in-one" (that is, at the footlights in front of a curtain that disguised the busy scene change behind it) was not working as a show-stopping number. One Saturday matinée, Bolger somehow went blank at the start of the second verse. Cy Feuer's seven-year-old son Bobby, who was in attendance and who knew the score by heart, prompted him—to the audience's delighted laughter and to Bolger's initial annoyance. But the cueing worked, as Bolger turned the moment into a singalong with the boy. From then on, Bolger embellished the number, playing games with the orchestra, provoking a musical climax, stopping, and then starting again. During the course of the Broadway run, the number grew in duration until by the closing night, it lasted twenty-five minutes!

The Broadway production received more criticism than praise. The *Herald Tribune* called it "a heavy-handed and witless entertainment." Brooks Atkinson branded it "mediocre" in the *Times*, calling the plot "pretty stupid." Ward Morehouse of the *Sun* thought Loesser's score was merely "routine" with only "a bright spot here and there." And Robert Coleman's headline in the *Daily Mirror* summed up the general feeling as it read: "Ray Bolger's Big Hit, But Where's Charley?" Only William

Hawkins of the *New York World Telegram* was wholly approving: "There is no point in fooling around about the fact. *Where's Charley?* is a sublimely satisfying evening."

At first, audiences seemed to share critics' reservations. Susan Loesser tells the story of a beautiful young woman asking her much older escort how he liked the show and being told, "Well, I liked it a lot better than *Medea.*"

But the show ran for two years on Broadway, went on tour with the original cast, and was made into a movie by Warner Brothers who bought the rights for $200,000—a significant sum in those days. Feuer and Martin were launched, but their challenge was to follow up this success with another.

One April afternoon in 1949, the partners were lolling about in the living room of an elegant, four-storey townhouse on East 64th Street in Manhattan. Puffing away on Cubana cigars, Martin was thumbing through a copy of Damon Runyon's stories, particularly the piece called "The Idyll of Miss Sarah Brown," when he suddenly exclaimed: "Gee! This stuff could be musicalized." With characteristic geniality, Feuer agreed: "You're darn tootin'!" Within two hours, they wired Frank Loesser to begin the songs, and Loesser, who was eagerly into woodworking as a hobby, found himself spending less time with clear pine or bird's-eye maple than he had planned. The *New York Times* reported on 12 May, 1949 that Loesser was set to score a musical based on Damon Runyon's Broadway stories.

But the rights to the stories were held by Paramount, which had already adapted *Little Miss Marker* into a Shirley Temple movie and had plans for further Runyon films. However, a deal was worked out between the studio and Feuer and Martin, whereby Paramount released the property in return for first refusal of screen rights to the stage production and twenty percent of film revenues. If the studio were to drop the rights, it would receive a twenty per cent discount.

By the third week of May, Martin was on his way to Hollywood to confer with Loesser and with Robert Carson who was working on a libretto. Martin and Feuer also hoped to land Ethel Merman but she proved unavailable owing to other commitments. A month later, Carson withdrew from the project in order to fulfill his obligation to Universal for the script of *Harvey*, and after trying out about half a dozen other writers, the producers hired Joseph (Jo) Swerling, a prominent and high-priced Hollywood screenwriter, whose long list of credits included *Made For Each Other, The Westerner, Blood and Sand, Pride of the Yankees, Lifeboat, Leave Her to Heaven*, and *It's A Wonderful Life*.

A Russian by birth, the fifty-two year old Swerling had begun his writing career by composing sketches for vaudeville. Experienced and versatile though he was, he was to find the Runyon project not quite his cup of tea. He completed his first act late in 1949: it was well-written and very much in the style Feuer and Martin had originally conceived for the show. The problem was that Feuer and Martin were having several changes of mind about the style.

There were publicity announcements about the start of rehearsals (early December, 1949 for a late January 1950 opening), negotiations in November, 1949 with Daniel Mann to direct, and attempts to lure Tony Martin (headlining at the Roxy) to play Sky. The singer wanted to do the show but on condition that the producers make a deal with MGM to let his wife, Cyd Charisse, come East and play a lead in it. "I've been away from home long enough and if we can't do something here together, I'm not going to do it alone," commanded the crooner. When Mann dropped out because of other commitments, the producers signed Jo Mielziner to design, light, and provide general direction. Almost two weeks later, Jerome Robbins was announced as choreographer, but his July calendar was filled, and the next April he was replaced by Michael Kidd. In January, 1950, Feuer, Martin, and Swerling were said to be huddling with Frank Sinatra to take a lead, then the next month the producers tried to land Robert Merrill from the Met, and managed to sign George Basserman, famous in Hollywood for work on *Cabin in the Sky, The Clock, The Postman Always Rings Twice,* and *The Wizard of Oz,* to score the musical arrangements. In May, Irene Sharaff was named to do costuming, a month after Robert Alda was reported to play a lead.

Meanwhile, the libretto was still proving a problem to the producers who recruited Peter Lyon and Abe Burrows to collaborate with Swerling. It was becoming increasingly clear to all concerned that Runyon was a difficult source to adapt, although it hadn't seemed that way at first.

Runyon's name was quite familiar to newspaper and magazine readers across the nation, for even before the Broadway stories carved his name for posterity in the same order (though not rank) of Mark Twain and Bret Harte, Damon Runyon had already been nationally celebrated as a very successful Hearst newspaper reporter, equally adept at covering sports, crime, politics, high society, and the low life. Of the estimated eighty million words that he wrote, most were uncollected in book form and remained scattered through the daily columns and Sunday features in such publications as the *Rocky Mountain News,* the *New York American, Daily Mirror,* and *Journal American.* The columns ran the gamut from news reports, editorial opinions, and poems to anecdotes, vignettes, and short features. But Runyon's largest claim to fame were his Broadway stories, and although he wrote about a variety of milieus (including the polo fields and penthouses at Parc Vendome, the courtrooms in Queens and Jersey, the white mansions in Florida, Hollywood, Pimlico, Hialeah, and Saratoga, and his native Wild West), his most vivid settings were from Broadway: Jack Dunstan's all-night eatery in prewar days, glittering nightclubs, sleazy speakeasies, and celebrity-packed Lindy's and Toots Shor's. Many of his fictional characters were modelled on real-life counterparts: Black Mike Marrio is more than a hint of Al Capone, who was Runyon's neighbour in Miami and who left him his prized whippets as a keepsake when he had to go to prison; Dave the Dude is a rough version of Frank Costello, who was a loyal fan; and Waldo Winchester is a free-hand caricature of Walter Winchell, the famous columnist and broadcaster with whom Runyon drove all over New York to uncover unusual crimes. But the cultural roots of Runyon had nothing to do with Broadway or the bright lights of a big city.

Born Alfred Damon Runyan in Manhattan, Kansas, on 8 October, 1880, he was the son of Alfred Lee Runyan, a red-haired, itinerant printer and publisher of small newspapers. The family name was a corruption of "Renoyan," a name whose genealogy went back to France in pre-Revolutionary days. His family background filled Damon with pride: "We come from a long line of Hugenot horse thieves who were run out of France by posses." Whether this stretched the truth or not, the claim revealed Runyon's love of adventure. The bare facts of his life are laid out clearly by Tom Clark in his introduction to *The Bloodhounds of Broadway.* Runyon's paternal grandfather, William Renoyan, an itinerant printer, was once the leader of a gold expedition in 1852 that found itself stranded on the dry Blue River of Kansas while seeking to discover an inland waterway to California. There the party founded the frontier village of Manhattan. Renoyan Americanized his surname to Runyan, started a local newspaper, and taught the printer's trade to his son, Alfred, who grew up to be a set of outrageous anomalies: Indian fighter in his youth when he packed a six-gun, lover of the classics, gambler, drunkard, and saloon orator. He married Elizabeth Damon, whose ancestry could be traced back to the Massachusetts Bay Colony. Elizabeth's health was destroyed by the rigours of bearing four children, her husband's business failures, and her own bouts of diphtheria and consumption. Alfred offered little comfort. Although a lover of the classics, he was an inveterate gambler and drunkard. The only concession he made to his wife was to move the family to Colorado, where the clear mountain air might alleviate his wife's health problems. But shortly after their arrival in 1887, she succumbed to tuberculosis, and Alfred dispatched his three daughters to Kansas where they could be raised by in-laws, while he took charge in his primitive way of Damon who, at the time, was scrawny and high-strung. Father and son roomed in a flophouse, and while the father attended to his business as printer for the Pueblo Chieftain, the boy had all the time in the world to run loose and bare-footed in the dirt streets of a town which was filled with bars, gambling houses, and bordellos. Young Damon frequently played hookey from school, and left to his own devices, he acquired a worldly education instead of a formal one. He dropped out of school at nine, recruited a gang or ran errands when he needed a dime, and stood at his father's side in a saloon to listen to Alfred's tall tales about Buffalo Bill Cody and Billy the Kid, and to his eclectic quotations from Shakespeare, the Scriptures, Confucius, and Montaigne.

It was a frontier life with a rough texture, but it gave Alfred Damon an early exposure to low life and the resources required to cope with and surmount it. The boy quickly followed his father's footsteps by becoming a printer's devil and then a junior reporter assigned to cover fires and hotel arrivals. He also wrote verse in imitation of Kipling, and then at fourteen he was assigned to cover a lynching—which would have turned the stomach of anyone not used to frontier justice. The next year, he acquired the status of a full-fledged reporter to accompany a more disreputable status as chain-smoker, whiskey-guzzler, and gun-toting barroom habitué.

A printer's error was responsible for his name-change to Runyon, but the teenage whiz—with a byline at seventeen in the Pueblo Evening Post—accepted it with perverse delight, for he regarded the change as a stamp of individuality that distinguished him from his father. His first name would later be dropped in a New York newspaper office, making him simply Damon Runyon, but not before a series of adventures which included serving as a teen infantryman in the Phillippines and in the Spanish American War, and later stealing rides on freight trains and moving through dangerous hobo "jungles" for six months.

He reported for the *Pueblo Chieftain* and then several other small newspapers, and in 1904 *Collier's Magazine* published his poem, "Song of the Bullet." Two years later, he reported sports for the *San Francisco Post* and then the *Rocky Mountain News*, and in 1907 had his first short story published in a national magazine. New York beckoned him, as it did any aspiring reporter, but when he did move there in 1910, his ambition was thwarted at first. It took him six months to be permitted inside an editor's door. This was a true newspaper world—there were over a dozen morning and afternoon papers—and Park Row was thought to be paradise. But the young man from the wild frontier quickly came to prominence as a sports reporter for the *New York American*, prompting William Randolph Hearst, the owner, to mark Runyon's pieces with a blunt copy pencil and to remark to his sub-editors: "This young man, whoever he is, seems to be making us money. Read what he writes!"

Runyon's excellent reporting was not limited to sports. He never turned down any assignment, whether is was the Giants training camp in Texas, the Madero revolution in Mexico, the First World War in Europe, or political conventions, prize fights, yacht races, and sensational murder trials. He yearned for anything exciting and colourful.

By the early 20s, he was earning $20,000 a year as syndicated feature writer, news reporter, and sports columnist for the Hearst empire. Spurred on by his success, he experimented with his prose, challenging his readers with more idiosyncratic writing. He was soon allowed to pick his baseball ass—ignments, though Hearst especially valued him for his coverage of politics and crime. Heady success sharpened Runyon's lust for journalism but did nothing for his marriage or children.

It wasn't long before he was ranked by peers in the company of Ring Lardner, although there were significant differences between the two. Lardner drank; Runyon did not. Lardner had success as a fiction writer; Runyon was still only a newspaperman. Lardner was attracted to the literary élite (F. Scott Fitzgerald, Edmund Wilson, and assorted company of the Algonquin Round Table); Runyon was drawn to figures such as Jimmy Walker, Al Capone, and Arnold Rothstein.

Runyon roared along in the twenties, beginning with his second biographical series on Jack Dempsey and ending the decade with newspaper parodies of detective stories and his first Broadway story, "Romance in the Roaring Forties," placed in *Cosmopolitan Magazine*. He and the jazz era were virtually in a symbiotic relationship. Prohibition merely catalyzed the popularity of illicit booze, sleazy cabaret, and underground vice. The twenties were the age of flappers who wanted "sugar" daddies and who didn't mind being thought of as gold-diggers. Runyon didn't mind their company, disguising his late-night liaisons with leggy chorus girls as research in "atmosphere" for his work. It was a half-truth, of course, but every rendezvous did fuel his story-telling imagination when it came to writing about his Broadway "guys and dolls." His characteristic habit of listening silently to others (a development, it seems, from his frontier childhood) served him well when it came to examining character through speech patterns. Moreover, his power of observation helped him evoke mood and setting in a few accurate phrases.

Runyon churned out verse, sketches, and short stories, and he became rich enough to own a stable of racehorses, a pack of hunting dogs, shares in some heavyweight boxers (including the bumbling giant, Primo Carnera), Upper West Side apartments where he kept his first wife (who turned to alcohol in her loneliness) and two sons (whom he rarely saw), and bachelor apartments closer to the Broadway life he relished.

The next decade represented Runyon at his peak, beginning with the publication of *Guys and Dolls*, his collection of Broadway stories, continuing with film versions and further collected editions, and ending with his new columns of opinion by a mythical father. Early in the decade, his estranged first wife, Ellen, died, but this sad event did not interfere with either his prodigious volume of writing or his appetite for luxurious living. Nor did it delay his marriage to a Silver Slipper show girl, Patrice Amati, a few months after Ellen's death.

Hollywood films were growing increasingly popular around the country, and Runyon became a devoted fan, seeing at least ten films a week. As his biographer, Tom Clark, claims: "The influence of movies on his writing, especially his fiction, was direct—and vice versa. Both Runyon and the Hollywood producers were looking for the kind of 'make 'em laugh, make 'em cry' story ingredients on which popular artistic success is always based." Runyon and the movies "always had the same thing in mind, and that was to entertain." His first movie sale, an unpublished story "The Geezer," occurred in 1927 to Universal Pictures, and earned him $5000, nearly a quarter of his annual reporter's salary at the time. Five years later, Frank Capra bought "Madame La Gimp" for Columbia for $35,000, and turned it into *Lady For a Day*, a movie that won Capra an Oscar as Best Director. (Fourteen years after Runyon's death, when Capra repurchased the rights from Columbia for a remake, *Pocketful of Miracles*, the price was $225,000!) Added to these impressive sales were those of his short stories to magazines such as Collier's, Cosmopolitan, and the Saturday Evening Post at rates as high as $5000 apiece.

Broad though his interests were in subject matter, Runyon was shrewd enough to realize that his Broadway stories were his gold mine. He was quoted as saying: "I took one little section of New York and made half a million writing about it." Readers enjoyed tales such as "Blonde Mink," "Butch Minds the Baby," "The Hottest Guy in the World," "Princess O'Hara," "The Melancholy Dane," and "Pick the Winner," which presented characters such as Julie the Starker (" a strong rough guy"), Miss Beatrice Gee (clothes-horse and ex-show girl), Little Isadore, Butch (former safecracker), Spanish John, Harry the Horse, Big Jule ("the hottest guy in the whole world"), Ambrose Hammer (a cynical drama critic), Hot Horse Herbie ("a tall, skinny guy with a most depressing kisser"), and Miss Cutie Singleton ("a little, good-natured blond doll"). Although the fictive elements were strong, most of the characters had an authenticity. Indeed, Heywood Broun remarked in his introduction to Guys and Dolls that the events and occurrences in the tales moved and excited him because he recognized "the various characters concerned as actual people who are at this moment living and loving, fighting and scuttling no more than a quarter of a mile from the place in which I live." Broun's comment suggested an aspect of social documentary in Runyon's stories, and there is no question that many of the colourful characters were derived from real-life figures, but the parallels between fiction and real life are insufficient to account for the enduring charm of the Broadway stories. Any plausible explanation of Runyon's claim to literary fame could not afford to overlook his settings, narrative point of view, comic characters, and his unique slang, which one of his critics fondly called "slanguage."

Heywood Broun, a great humorist himself, observed that every story in the first edition of *Guys and Dolls* "can be located as having its principal routes somewhere between Times Square and Columbus Circle." The parameter is thereby far narrower than the settings in O'Henry or Twain, but the geography of *Guys and Dolls* is precise and colourful, while providing the pleasure of easy recognition. It is largely a neon world, with the bright lights of Broadway that excite most tourists and visitors to the Big Apple. But Runyon doesn't expend much time on description or scene-painting. Place-names, dialogue, and action are what bring the locales to life in broad, vivid strokes.

His characters, too, are evoked with a few strokes. In a method that can be traced back to Smollett, Dickens, and Twain, Runyon creates comedy of humors through monikers and physiognomy. There is no subtlety, or depth in characters such as Nicely-Nicely, Nathan Detroit, Sky Masterson, Miss Adelaide, or Miss Sarah Brown. Their names are emblems of their personalities or quirks of temperament and behaviour. They are caricatural but effectively dramatic, sentimental, or comic—perhaps chiefly because of the skillful narrative whose gentle comic tone we can also find in Stephen Leacock. Patricia Ward D'Itri has described the anonymous narrator as a minor character, a faceless, nameless figure who just happens to be a hanger-on in various places and at various times. Probably a projection of Runyon himself, he sometimes participates in action that he describes, but even when he is simply a recounter of tales, he assumes the air of an innocent, subject to exaggeration and colourful slang. Frederick T. Marsh called him "an unforgettable mug in the rogue's gallery of fiction," approving of his half-boob air and "pawky" way of telling a story. "He is a wit, a story teller, an ironist, a wise guy looking to keep out of trouble, a small-timer hanging on the fringes of big-shot life, tolerated because he's a humorist and a tower of strength, with his fine baritone in impromptu harmoniz ing after the shooting (he always ducks) is over. As he says himself, he's known to one and all as a guy who is just around."

But the narrator is especially effective because of his grammar, syntax, and slang. He uses the present tense to create a sense of immediacy, spontaneity, and theatricality. The device was something Runyon developed into a signature style, and its roots obviously went back to his childhood, youth, and newspaper apprenticeship. In Pueblo, persons of little education and no sophistication recounted events in the present tense. Runyon encountered similar usage among hoboes, army personnel in barracks, and underworld figures. While grammatically primitive and syntactically infelicitous, the device allows the reader to witness action as it unfolds. The uninterrupted sense of time, where there is no future (whether perfect, imperfect, or indefinite), allows the narrative to flow on and build like a wave. A vivid demonstration of this can be had by listening to Jerry Orbach's narration of some of the stories in *Guys and Dolls*, where the actor's voice has to be strong and supple enough to accommodate the pace and volume of words without affording the luxury of many pauses. Indeed, the pauses only come when the actor-narrator needs to take a deep breath before resuming the verbal sequence.

Such abundance would result in tedium were it not for Runyon's highly original slang that convincingly creates a distinctive ambience. The slang is eclectic: as Patricia Ward D'Itri shows, it combines a few French and British words, a little Yiddish, some Biblical terms, and the argot of sub-groups such as hoboes, journalists, and gamblers. So the mixture becomes richly peculiar but highly comic as "cops" meet the "gendarme" as they go after a *gonoph* (Yiddish for "thief"). Much of the humor is obtained from slang variations such as "old equalizer" or "rooty-toot-toot" for "gun." As D'Itri notes, the slang shows other flexibility as when it grows ramified to demarcate specific denominations of money— slugs ($1), fins ($5), saw bucks ($10), yards ($100), half yards ($50), and G's ($1000)—or when it connotes double meanings, as in "marker" (which would mean an IOU or a tombstone) or as in "give someone a chill" (which may mean to slight or kill a person). Synecdoche is used with orginality, as in "tongue" for lawyer, "The Beard" for Uncle Sam, and "the Gideon" for the Bible. And Runyon makes especially effective use of under-world jargon, such as "jug" (bank), "pete" (safe), "pokey" (jail), "damper" (cash register), "cheaters" (guns), "croak" (die), "dukes" (fists), "kisser" (mouth), "shiv" (knife), and "monkey business" (which needs no translation). Runyon's clever idiosyncrasies with grammar and slang created a style that has, unfortunately, been imitated by countless journalists and critics who never quite match his sharp humour or fresh-ness.

Three of Runyon's stories were especially appealing to Feuer and Martin when they were discussing the possibility of a musical. Their main interest was in "The Idyll of Miss Sarah Brown," but they also had a good look at "Pick The Winner" and "Blood Pressure." The result was an idea for a very Runyonesque plot, replete with gangsters, dolls, and an entire corps of assorted figures culled from the busy passing parade between Times Square and Columbus Circle.

The main characters, as Feuer, Martin, and Jo Swerling dec–ided, were to be gamblers Nathan Detroit and Sky Masterson, with their respective "dolls," Miss Adelaide and Sarah Brown, but the main plot revolved around Sky's romancing the sober, puritanical Save-a-Soul Mission lass. The fundamental anomaly of such a pairing did not bother either the producers or Swerling. Salvation Army heroines were not strictly anathema to either the legitimate theatre or to the musical stage, as was already proved by the successes of *Major Barbara* and *The Belle of New York*. Perhaps, too, it was fair to speculate that there was something deliciously perverse in mixing religion and sex.

The problem lay with the mode of adaptation. Runyon's style, though essentially oral and informal, works better on the printed page than as theatre dialogue. Moreover, Runyon's world is a coded one—"as hermetic, consistent and original as Wodehouse's or Flann O'Brien's," in the words of Richard Eyre—and the difficulty for a stage adaptor was to present this larger-than-life world without parody or facetiousness.

As Jo Swerling plodded on manfully with the libretto, Feuer and Martin were convinced that the show could work on the same romantic level as *South Pacific*. By uttering the magic word "Runyon," they were able to recruit Frank Loesser for the score. After a few months of collaborating with Swerling, Loesser realized all was not well. His songs were being composed with his usual skill and the basic outline of the story was fine, but Swerling's book didn't seem to have the right tone or pace.* For one thing, Swerling was sticking slavishly to Runyon without inventing fresh material to make the transition from page to stage seem effortless. For another, the libretto wasn't really funny, and Runyon without real humour seemed pallid, especially for musical comedy.

There needed to be a new direction.

---

*One of Loesser's songs that survives in its original draft version reveals the the lighter and more lyrical musical that was first conceived. What became the famous "Fugue for Tinhorns" started as "Three-Cornered Tune," and its opening lines convey some of the romantic mood of the musical that was to be based chiefly on "The Idyll of Miss Sarah Brown": "It has a tender sound/This little tune I found/I don't know why/It's following me around." Sarah Brightman sings it in her lovely soprano on *The Songs that Got Away* (produced by Andrew Lloyd Webber and Marvin Hamlisch for The Really Useful Record Co. Ltd., 839 116-4 Stereo, 1989).

*Guys and Dolls* (1950)

# LIFE OF THE PARTY

**ABE BURROWS** set the correct direction for the book, although he did not have the right omens at first. One night after dinner at Cy Feuer's home in New York, Loesser played and sang some of the numbers from the show for the producers, and Burrows and his wife, Carin. They were "enchanting," thought Burrows who felt, however, that "they would be effective no matter who sang them." In other words, they were not individualized or defined enough to be thoroughly true to a specific character in the story. Then Loesser played a brand-new song of his that was not intended for the show. Called " Forever," it was "a satirical, amusing but slightly bitter love song" that Burrows felt would fit perfectly into *Guys and Dolls*. Ernest Martin did not share his view at all, and was particularly annoyed that Burrows would comment on a project that was none of his business. Martin raised his voice in sharp disagreement. He didn't see *Guys and Dolls* as a hilarious satirical comedy, and the more Burrows held to his view, the angrier Martin grew. Finally, sounding to Burrows "like a judge pronouncing sentence," he said, "Abe, if you are a man who thinks that that song is right for *Guys and Dolls*, you could never be the man to write *Guys and Dolls*."

Knowing full well that nobody had so far been able to write a satisfactory script, Burrows laughed, "Ernie, I never planned to write it, and now you're already firing me." Then he apologized for sticking his nose into what was not his own business, but he couldn't resist one more wisecrack: "However, Ernie, don't ever close the door."

A few months later, Martin "opened the door." He visited Burrows to recruit him. Burrows respected the fact that Martin and his partner were risking considerable money and their reputation on the venture. He knew that the producers had changed their minds about the predominant tone of the show: they now wanted a comedy. Loesser agreed with them, even though this radical tonal shift increased the risk for the producers who had already raised a great deal of money from their backers on the strength of Jo Swerling's first act and the fourteen songs Frank Loesser had finished.

Feuer and Martin worked out a settlement with Swerling who agreed to withdraw from the project on condition that he retain a diminished royalty and the right to read the final script and to determine what billing, if any, he should get himself. It was a delicate situation because Swerling and Burrows knew each other. But a deal was arranged that satisfied Swerling and the Dramatists Guild, and Abe Burrows, the erudite funnyman, was a new part of the *Guys and Dolls* team.*

Burrows had known Feuer as a fellow-student at New Utrecht High School and Martin as the man who had pushed him into becoming a performer. Then, too, Loesser was one of his dearest friends, and Michael Kidd, who had just been hired to choreograph the show, had also attended New Utrecht. So there was a network of connections. Burrows also realized that he had been subconsciously working on the show ever since he heard Loesser's songs at Feuer's dinner party. After a short spell to think over the offer, Burrows accepted.

When Loesser heard the news, he phoned from California and burbled: "You'll be great." "Thanks, Frank, I'm going to try to make it as funny as I can." There was a brief pause before Loesser said: "Abe...not *too* funny." Did Loesser simply mean that he didn't want to be burdened with silly gags or the radio humour that was Burrows' specialty? Or did he mean that he wanted something else to tinge the comedy? Or was it that Loesser was simply tired about his reputation as a writer of comic songs and was aiming at something else? Burrows was to understand only in 1956 when, after raving about the marvellously funny songs in *The Most Happy Fella*, Loesser cut him off angrily: "Abe, the hell with that! We both know I can do that kinda stuff. Tell me where I made you cry."

Eager to take over the libretto, Burrows was quite prepared to accept advice from the producers, Loesser, and the eventual director. After all, this was his first Broadway show, and although he already had a solid reputation as a song-journalist and radio-writer, he knew that no Broadway musical ever gets to final form without the librettist's collaboration with colleagues from other production areas. He had distinctive credentials for a Runyon adaptation. For one thing, he was instinctively droll, deeply grained in contemporaneity which put him in the company of Groucho Marx, Fred Allen, Robert Benchley, and George S. Kaufman. For another, he was a native New Yorker who had worked his way to wide popular and critical acceptance in his various capacities as radio writer and performer, nightclub entertainer, and composer. A third factor was his easy alliance with song, even though he sang in a gravelly baritone and his piano technique was thought quite imp–ossible by José Iturbi. However, his gift for parody demonstrated an acute ear for rhythm, the contours of melody, and the shape of a lyric.

Born Abram Borowitz on December 8, 1910 in the Lower East Side of Manhattan, he had Russian forefathers. When he and his family moved to the Bronx (then considered "the suburbs"), he lived the same side of the street as Sholem Aleichem who spent his last years there. However, Aleichem was not as famous to the younger Borowitz as was Mrs. Leonard, the mother of Benny Leonard, the Jewish Light Heavyweight Champion of the World. The next family move was to Brooklyn. Burrows attended New Utrecht whose eventual claim to fame was that it was *alma mater* to many who became big names in show business, such as opera star Robert Merrill, comedians Phil Foster and Buddy Hackett, producer Cy Feuer, and choreographer Michael Kidd. Burrows obviously inherited some of his father's love of the entertainment world, for Louis, who ran wallpaper and paint concessions in various Brooklyn department stores, was a great fan of vaudeville and probably a frustrated entertainer. There was always a piano around the house, and Burrows and his four brothers and five sisters would sing, dance, and entertain themselves, putting on a little show for themselves. He sometimes bet all comers a nickel apiece that he could recall at least the tune, if not the lyric as well, of any song from any musical that had ever run on Broadway for more than a month.

Burrows distinguished himself academically in Latin, so much so that he was able to serve as tutor and turn himself into a devotee of classical etymology. His mother wanted him to become a doctor, but he dropped out of pre-med City College in order to serve as a runner on Wall Street at $12 a week so that he could afford, he lied, to study accounting in the evening. His real interest was far from the world of stock certificates, shares, bonds, or balanced accounts, although he did serve as board boy before losing his job in 1933 owing to the nation's perilous economy. He was forced to accept work as a salesman of woven labels, but his penchant for jokes was never quashed and it was not long before he was put in touch with joke-writer Frank Galen, and so given a partner in hilarity. The two didn't take show business by storm, though they did sell jokes at $2 apiece to Irving (Swifty) Lazar who represented Henny Youngman. They also wrote material for Eddie Cantor's vaudeville act and for other comedians. Their luck increased when they met Ed Gardner who produced the CBS radio show, *This Is New York*. In the summer of 1939, Gardner, who was asked to produce *Texaco Star Theatre*, hired Galen and Burrows for the staff of this half-hour show starring comedian Ken Murray, singers Frances Langford and Kenny Baker, and various guest stars. For almost the next six years, everything Burrows did was on radio for Gardner whose feelings about comedy writing were influenced by his admiration for stage dialogue. When Gardner produced and starred in a half-hour pilot about Archie, a New York mug who constantly talked about a salon-keeper called Duffy, this marked the beginning of what was to become *Duffy's Tavern*, for which Burrows wrote such accurate dialogue that Damon Runyon was prompted to send him a note of admiration.

Off the air, Burrows was proving no less engaging at comic improvisations. Once described as "a hefty pixie," he had a large, wide girth. Six feet, one inch in height, he had a large bald head, small feet, and eyes that blinked spasmodically behind jutting spectacles. He performed at parties, sending up pop tunes and titles with absurd flourish, such as in his song "Memory Lane" where he sang of "strolling down memory lane without a goddam thing on my mind," or as in another song which lamented "You put a piece of carbon paper under your heart and gave me just a copy of your love." Despite his takeoffs, he didn't alienate fellow songwriters who loved to gather around the piano while he was improvising and knock themselves out with laughter. "After a while I realized each of them thought I was kidding some other songwriter's work. Of course, they may also have sensed that in an odd way I was paying them a compliment because, after all, you can't put across a parody unless whatever it is you're parodying is already popular. The imitation depends for its effect on the strength of the original." By way of illustration, he pointed out that in vaudeville if you wanted a big hand, you did an impression of

Al Jolson, but it was really Jolson's fame and genius that got you the applause. Burrows liked to quote Max Beerbohm's epigram, "Satire is based on qualified love."

Burrows' party improvisations became the stuff of local legend. Harry Kunitz, author of *Reclining Figures* and a humorist of distinction himself, claimed that hearing Burrows do his own material for the first time was "one of the funniest experiences a human being can have." New York hostesses would even go to the bother of renting a piano for the impromptu performer who couldn't read music. Burrows and Marc Connelly once improvised an hour-long, non-stop burlesque of a Shubert operetta, and fellow guests found Burrows' titles alone worthy of merry applause because they were so deadly funny: "I Drew a Foul Ball in the Pennant Race of Love," "Oh, How We Danced on the Night We Were Wed; I Needed a Wife Like a Hole in the Head," "Darling, Why Shouldn't You Look Well Fed, You Ate Up a Hunk of My Heart," "Riding Through the Cactus, I Got Stuck On You."

It was at one of these antic parties that he first met Frank Loesser in 1943. On army furlough, Loesser reluctantly yielded to his wife's urging to meet Burrows at a Beverly Hills celebration. When Burrows broke into an impromptu song, "The Girl with the Three Blue Eyes," he fractured Loesser for life. "It was clear to me," joked Loesser, "that Abe Burrows was the greatest living American." So impressed was Loesser, in fact, that he was able to sing back the exact lyric to Burrows (who had forgotten it) when he surprised him the next day by a social telephone call.

Burrows quickly became the most sought-after guest on the West Coast, especially at functions hosted by Nunnally Johnson and Louis B. Mayer. Towards the end of the war, when Loesser was transferred to New York, he hosted a party in honour of Burrows at Hotel Novarro. Burrows was still in California, but Loesser introduced him to guests by telephone as Burrows wisecracked: "We're having a party here, too, and we're running out of ice. Send some over."

As a playing guest, Burrows attended half a dozen parties a week, many at homes of people he hardly knew. To many, he was a social lion—something he once wittily described as "a person who is usually asked to make up for the bad food." Burrows was wise enough to assess his own role as party entertainer. In a 1957 *New Yorker* profile, he was quoted as saying: "When I became a party fellow, I was a frustrated entertainer. I was making a good living writing for radio, but I needed an outlet—a satisfaction. I was unfulfilled, and I think this is true of most so-called lives of the party."

Ernest Martin, then a radio producer, heard some of the party patter and songs and (with the help of Joan Davis, star of a hit radio show) tricked Burrows into going on the air and performing. Burrows was a smash hit. In 1947 CBS decided to give him his own show, consisting of him and an instrumental quartet, and directed by Carin Smith, the woman who was to become his wife. Early in 1949 he signed what *Variety* called "an exclusive seven-year, four-way contract with CBS." The "four-way" part referred to his functions as performer, producer, director, and writer. He joined a new CBS panel show, *This Is Broadway*, which later became a hit TV show called *This Is Show Business*. He also started a new weekly half-hour radio program that because it went on at nine in the evening had the droll title *Breakfast With Burrows (He Gets Up Late)*. That was not all: he starred in a TV show called *The Abe Burrows Almanac* after his radio show failed to catch fire, and he was a panellist on TV's *We Take Your Word* about the derivation of words, a subject that had been dear to him ever since his schooldays. When *The Abe Burrows Almanac* was dropped, he was assigned to write and produce a half-hour TV show five days a week called *The Stork Club* (because it originated from the Stork Club).

He had Yul Brynner for a director, and Peter Lind Hayes, Mary Healy, and the club's owner, Sherman Billingsley, as his stars.

It was a hectic schedule—even for a comic genius—which became even more hectic when he began his work on *Guys and Dolls*. Burrows wanted to transcend parody because that gift came too easily to him and was turning him (in his own words) into "a kind of parasite." He was wearying of having to look through *Variety* every week, hoping to find that someone had turned out a "simply awful" song just so that he could "rib" it. The *Guys and Dolls* libretto needed a different sort of genius, one that was original enough to take a slight story and fatten it up with richly comic characters and situations that were true to the spirit and almost breathless pace of the Runyon source-material.

But before he could tackle the libretto, Burrows had to deal with other stresses. CBS had contracted entitlement to his exclusive services, so in order to appease the legal department he took a cut in salary with the additional understanding that much of the Runyon work would have to be done in his spare time. Even trickier than the CBS situation was the matter of Feuer and Martin's backers. Raising money for the show was difficult because neither the book nor director had been finalized. Music Corporation of America, called "the octopus of the entertainment world," had taken the biggest piece of investment—a $16,000 chunk—while Tony Farrell, a chronic "angel," was the largest individual investor. Music publisher Edwin H. Morris put in $10,000; and Feuer $8,000, as did recording executive, Mamie Sacks. Martin was good to the tune of $6,000, whereas most of the other backers (who included Louis A. Lotito, President of City Playhouses, Inc.; ad exec William H. Weintraub; Metro producer Armand S. Deutsch; actress Helen Menken; Frank Loesser; Mrs. Jo Swerling; Mrs. Jo Mielziner; former entrepreneur Billy Rose; and the dentist of Vivian Blaine's husband, Manny Frank) threw in small shares at $4,000 a unit.

When word got out that Burrows, who had no theatre record, was working on a new libretto, some of these backers grew nervous. One of them was Billy Rose who, though counting Burrows as a friend, didn't let friendship interfere with business. He demanded a return of his investment. Ernie Martin asked Burrows to phone Rose and help him change his mind, but after Burrows had presented an eminently reasonable case in his own defence as librettist, Rose responded: "Kid, you're a good friend of mine and I know you're a great comedy writer, but you've never done a Broadway show." The upshot, plain and simple, was that he wanted his money back.

(At a dinner party during the second year of the show's run on Broadway, Oscar Hammerstein II would congratulate Burrows on his success and would remark to Rose: "Hey, Billy, I'm sure you got a big piece of it." Before Burrows could even blink in his customary way, Rose replied with a straight face: "No, Oscar, I didn't put any money into it because I didn't know Abe was going to write it.")

"Green and frightened" was how Burrows described his own feelings as a neophyte Broadway librettist. He requested a collaborator, so Ernest Martin brought in Peter Lyon. The partnership fizzled out after a couple of weeks owing to a combination of Burrows' TV schedule and his own uncertainty about a clear path for the book. He decided that he needed "to start fresh and go it alone."

Of course, he wasn't really alone. He would consult with Loesser (who was in California) by phone and with the co-producers. He "leaned" on Cy Feuer heavily, working nightly on the first draft with him. "Feuer was a fine musician and that was very important because Frank Loesser's songs were the guideposts for the libretto. It's a rare show that's done this way." But because Loesser's songs were all wonderful, the libretto had to be so constructed that the story would lead organically into each of them. Burrows wrote in his autobiography: "The word integration usually means that the composer has written songs that follow the story line gracefully. Well, we accomplished that but we did it in reverse. Most of the scenes I wrote blended into songs that were already written."

He would comment in a 1961 New York Post interview that as a satirist, he found the musical to be his form. "I don't think satire can work in straight theater, at least in this country. In France, Giraudoux and Anouilh use satire in the straight play, but for some reason the American audience wants music with its satire....Maybe it's because with music you're not hitting them directly; so they can listen and subconsciously absorb."

Burrows also knew that every song by Loesser fit beautifully into the structure of the story. When the show became an established hit on Broadway, making it difficult for even Burrows to buy tickets, he would repeat the secret of Guys and Dolls: Everything goes together. "Nothing is in there that doesn't belong. There are no love ballads which are written in a different language from the dialogue. When a mug sings a love song, it's a mug type love song. The dances are strictly in character. There's a crap game ballet which looks like a crap game. A real Runyon crap game. In this show we didn't care about how a single number or scene would go....We cared about the whole show and nothing went in unless it fit.

---

*Jo Swerling, Jr. has taken exception to the claim that Abe Burrows was the principal writer. In a letter to the New York Times on May 3, 1992, he wrote: "The book was written, the money was raised, and the show was cast and in rehearsal with the director before Burrows started on the project. He was brought in, with my father's permission (a requirement under Dramatists Guild rules) to snap up the dialogue, and he did just that. He did what in my end of the business would be defined as polish."

But such revisionism did not pass muster with Feuer and Martin, who responded with their own letter on May 31: "Swerling and other writers made valiant but vain efforts to articulate our concept of the Damon Runyon material we had purchased. But Abe Burrows wrote the script that is on the stage....A few days before the opening in Philadelphia, Burrows' finished script was sent to Swerling. Because Abe had written every word, we had already presented the Playbill copy for the Shubert Theater in Philadelphia, which read, 'Book by Abe Burrows.' To our dismay and to the shock of Frank Loesser, who wrote the score, and George S. Kaufman, who directed, we got a telegram from Swerling's agent demanding billing. We had no choice but to comply."

Swerling's billing offended Abel Green, editor of the weekly Variety, who, in a lengthy piece, pointed out Swerling's violation of an "author's code of ethics."

Even Kaufman's daughter, Anne Kaufman Schneider, got into the exchange, writing to confirm Burrows' work on the script with her father in Bucks County, Pa.

Feur and Martin remain adamantly loyal to Burrows. Their New York Times letter concluded with this chant: "Sue us. Sue us./Shoot bullets through us./We love Abe!"

## GUYS AND DOLLS

| | |
|---|---|
| Music and Lyrics: | Frank Loesser |
| Book: | Able Burrows, based on stories by Damon Runyon |
| Director: | George S. Kaufman |
| Cast: | Sam Levene, Robert Alda, Vivian Blain, Isabel Bigley, Stubby Kaye, Pat Rooney Sr., B.S. Pully, Tom Pedi, Peter Gennaro, Onna White, Buddy Shwab |
| New York Run: | 46th Street Theater; November 24, 1950; 1,200 |

# THE MOST INVENTIVE FELLA

**THE NUCLEUS** of the book was "The Idyll of Miss Sarah Brown," where big-time gambler Sky Masterson falls in love with a Salvation Army missionary who, in turn, converts him from his wicked ways. This love story was counterpointed by the wryly comic one of Nathan Detroit, proprietor of the "oldest established permanent floating crap game in New York," who is engaged to Miss Adelaide, leading lady at the Hot Box Club and victim of a psychosomatic illness on account of their frustrating long-term engagement. Other characters included portly Nicely-Nicely Johnson, gun-toting Big Jule from East Cicero, Illinois, and dice-players with funny names such as Harry the Horse, Angie the Ox, Benny Southstreet, and Rusty Charlie.

In Burrows' libretto, Sky and Sarah match the Runyon originals, although there are some alterations. Runyon's handsome Sky hails from "a little town in southern Colorado where he learns to shoot craps, and play cards, and one thing and another." His Christian name, Obadiah, has a biblical resonance, but apart from this and his familiarity with the Gideon bible (which he comes across in various hotels on his gambling itinerary), he has no real connection to religion. He lives by his wits, and takes to heart his father's advice about not being suckered into bets that will only embarrass him. He looks as innocent as a baby, but he is "smarter than three Philadelphia

lawyers." Masterson is such a compulsive gamber that he re-
fuses to take penicillin when ill because of a bet of ten C's that
his temperature will rise to 104!

His romantic interest is his moral foil. In Runyon, Sarah
Brown has "a first-class shape" and "one-hundred-per-cent
eyes in every respect," and she reacts angrily to Sky's mercenary motive behind winning Brandy Bottle Bates' soul for her.
She retaliates by gambling on the same terms as Sky uses with
others, and she has a sharp tongue as she wields the dice. She
has edge and is not as sentimental or romantic as the musical's
Sarah who goes off with Sky and gets comically drunk in Havana. According to Burrows, Runyon based his Sarah on "a gorgeous former Follies girl who became a missionary and devoted her life to converting the evil sinners and wicked gamblers who inhabited the Broadway theatrical district. Her looks
and style drew large, admiring crowds." Walter Winchell once
claimed to have been in love with her.

The musical Sarah is given a scene in which she gets drunk
and sings a rapturous ballad ("If I Were A Bell") that prompts
a conscience-ridden Sky to warn her not to get mixed up with
a guy like him. But the irony is that although Sky firmly places
"dolls" a distant second to "aces back to back," he capitulates
to his mission "doll."

The Nathan Detroit and Miss Adelaide of the musical are
based on Hot Horse Herbie and Miss Cutie Singleton in "Pick
The Winner." Herbie is "a tall skinny guy with a most depressing kisser" and is so nicknamed because "he is a tout who can
always tell you about a horse that is so hot it is practically on
fire...although sometimes Herbie's hot horses turn out to be
so cold they freeze everybody within fifty miles of them."

Herbie has promised for the past ten years to marry Miss
Cutie, a good-natured blonde, who yearns for "a little white
house with green shutters and vines all around and about."
But Herbie always successfully manages to evade marriage—

always until a respectable, tall, spindly professor from Princeton appears on the scene at a Miami racetrack. Hot Horse Herbie, who gets his ever-loving fiancee to masquerade as a fortune-teller, attempts to dupe Professor Woodhead into betting a packet on one of Cutie's fraudulent predictions. This makes for a hilarious set-piece in which Cutie gets carried away by her own masquerade. In a neat comic twist, the professor, spinning his own ingenious interpretation of her concocted rubbish, wins big at the track, thereby getting Miss Cutie to elope with him to Palm Beach where, presumably, she can finally get her chance at the sort of community property she has dreamed of.

The musical equivalents of Hot Horse Herbie and Miss Cutie are funnier and more carefully textured. Nathan Detroit is a dice-addict with a remarkable ability to wangle a location for "the oldest established permanent floating crap game in New York," and he is as vulnerable, though not as foolish, as Hot Horse Herbie. Although he is skilled in stretching out his engagement to Miss Adelaide, he does genuinely love his show "doll." And Miss Adelaide is far funnier and more touching than Miss Cutie. Her psychosomatic cold (induced by her inability to get Nathan to tie the knot) and her dumb sweetness make her endearing, as when she brushes aside Nathan's failure to get her a fourteenth "anniversary" gift: "I kinda like it when you forget to give me presents. It makes me feel like we're married."

Adelaide writes letters to her mother, spinning a fantasy of married life and motherhood, and inventing five fantasy children because her absent mother believes in big families. This is her form of hopefulness. But what makes her even more richly comic than this fantasy is her manner of speech. She attempts to sound sophisticated even as she keeps being betrayed by bad grammar.

Love does finally join these two together, although Nathan's moral reformation is not as plausible as Sky's. But then, as Sky remarks as if he knew all about the conventions of musical comedy, "Life is one big crap game, and the devil is using loaded dice!"

The supporting characters in Guys and Dolls are divertingly diverse. They come from various Runyon stories, and all have a refreshing humanity.

Nicely-Nicely Johnson is a transformation of the Nicely-Nicely Jones from "A Piece of Pie." Runyon's original is five feet eight inches tall, five feet nine inches wide, and possibly "the greatest eater in all history" who would give an elephant a photo-finish in an eating contest. Benny Southstreet is a version of the hustler in "A Nice Price," a story set in New London, Connecticut, and whose cast includes Sam the Gonoph, a sour-faced ticket speculator, and Liverlips, another of "the nickname-is-all" hustlers.

Two of the other most vivid supporting characters in the musical are Harry The Horse and Big Jule, with the former deftly sketched in "Butch Minds The Baby" (about a safe-cracking gambit that almost completely backfires), and the latter given notorious prominence in "The Hottest Guy In The World," where he is "hotter than a forty-five": "You can see that Big Jule is really very hot, what with the coppers all over the country looking for him high and low. In fact, he is practically on fire." In the musical, Big Jule is "a gorilla," intimidating enough to con everyone at the crap game into letting him win with blank dice, but this characterization derives from Rusty Charley's in "Blood Pressure," where Charley is "a big wide guy" and called "a gorilla, because he is known to often carry a gun in his pants pocket, and sometimes to shoot people down as dead as door nails with it if he does not like the way they wear their hats." Burrows copies some of the crap game action straight out of "Blood Pressure," but whereas Runyon stages his game over a garage in Fifty-second Street, Burrows sets his in an underground tunnel. Burrows also uses Runyon's idea of blank dice in order to expand Big Jule's bold-faced trumpery.

Frank Loesser had originally written scores of numbers for this Broadway underworld, but had discarded most of these for various reasons, chief of which was the fact that they simply didn't meet his own high standards. But the final score of seventeen songs and some instrumentals represented (in the words of Goddard Lieberson, soundtrack album producer) "a kind of 'total' of Frank Loesser" because it contained "almost every kind of song in his kit." And the kit was impressive, indeed, containing everything from tender romantic ballads and burlesque-house songs to fugues, recitatives, hymns, cantatas, and songs that artfully fused different musical styles.

In short, Loesser was a song-writing sensation who never worried about posterity. He simply wanted music and lyric to serve a particular function. His genealogy augured well for him musically. He was born in 1910 on upper Broadway to a German father who taught piano and a Czechoslovakian mother who had a dazzling mind. Music and lyrics seemed to come naturally to young Frank. He wrote his first song at the age of six, "The May Party," which celebrated the children's processions he watched in Central Park. At seven, he used to compose words, "in the best New York slang of the day" (claimed Life magazine) "to the rhythm of the elevated trains that passed through his neighborhood. One set of lyrics for the locals and another for the expresses." Everything suggested music: the chirp of crickets in chorus, steamboat whistles, even political oratory. He couldn't explain how he became a songwriter or how he composed, except to say that tunes and lyrics just popped into his head. "Of course your head has to be arranged to receive them. Some people's heads are arranged so that they keep getting colds. I keep getting songs." Unfortunately, his father died when Frank was fifteen, forcing Frank's mother to earn a living by translating novels and becoming a lecturer on current literature to various ladies' groups. Loesser's much elder brother, Arthur, was a musical prodigy who began giving concert tours at eighteen and who eventually became the head of the piano department at the Cleveland Institute of Music, as well as a highly regarded critic and musicologist. So, Frank, according to his daughter's memoir, grew up in a house "full of music and seething intellects. But he was a rebel from the beginning." At the age of two, he refused to speak German (once considered "the vehicle of culture"), the family's official language. He was later expelled from Townsend Harris Hall, an exclusive high school for gifted children, because he devoted more time to practical jokes than to his studies. He somehow managed to get accepted by City College of New York, but met with expulsion again, shortly after his entrance, because he failed every subject but English and gymnastics and because he had defiled a bronze statue. "I wasn't in the mood to learn" was his curt explanation.

It was obvious that his path in life was to be different from that of his brother, Arthur, who dazzled the European gentry with erudition and virtuoso classical piano pieces. Most of the family's income depended on Arthur's concert tours and teaching, but Frank also helped out by undertaking a long series of odd jobs, supplemented by early songwriting efforts. He sold classified ads for the *Herald Tribune*, drew political cartoons for the *Tuckahoe Review*, served as knit-goods editor for *Women's Wear* and as food-checker for a chain of restaurants. He was also city editor of the short-lived *New Rochelle News*, a process server, and screwer of lids for insecticide cans. But his goal was always to become a Tin Pan Alley composer.

According to his brother, who is quoted in the book *They're Playing Our Song*, Frank first displayed his talent as a lyricist one night when he was assigned by the New Rochelle paper to cover a Lions Club dinner. "He obliged an officer by supplying couplets celebrating the exploits of all the club members. Such lines as 'Secretary Albert Vincent, Read the minutes—right this instant,' got him started on his eventual career with words."

His penchant for lyrics had begun in his teens, and some of his earliest collaborators had been a group of friends who frequented the In Old Algiers restaurant on upper Broadway. His first real job as songwriter was with the Tin Pan Alley firm of Leo Feist. He was supposed to write lyrics for Joseph Brandfon's melodies at a salary of $40 a week. However, none of these songs was either used or published, and at the end of the year Loesser found himself dismissed from the company. He and William Schuman (who later became an esteemed classical composer) teemed with ideas for popular songs. They were sometimes hired as "special material writers" for acts, alternating responsibilities for words and music. However, their one published song, "In Love with a Memory of You," was a flop. But this setback did not deter Loesser from acquiring a "brassy New York blue-collar accent," sprinkled with ethnic idioms. He knew that Tin Pan Alley was dominated by New York Jews, and he aimed directly at their professional company.

At twenty-four, he came under the influence of Carey Morgan, who produced vaudeville acts and composed songs for them. Morgan was familiar with all kinds of music and had a pragmatic attitude towards tunes. Loesser told Ernest Havemann of *Life* magazine: "I used to sit in his studio and listen to him play opera on the piano, with running comments as he went along. I'll never forget the day he was playing the opera *Tosca* for me. When he got to the crucial part, he said, 'Now listen carefully here. This is where they kill the S.O.B.'"

Loesser recognized that a good lyric is one of the most difficult art forms in the world. His early failures were partial evidence of this. But he also knew that he had a genius for lyric-writing and really needed the right break.

By the mid-thirties, he flirted with success. "Junk Man" did not bring immediate fame, but "I Wish I Were Twins" was recorded by Fats Waller in 1934. The next year, Loesser teamed up with Irving Actman in a New York nightclub, the Back Drop, and the following year they contributed songs to the Broadway revue, *The Illustrators Show*, which was damned by reviewers. The pair returned to the Back Drop where Loesser met his wife-to-be, singer Lynn Garland. Soon after, Loesser and Actman were discovered by a movie studio scout, leading to a six-month Hollywood contract with Universal Studios.

Universal had the right to "adapt, arrange, change, transpose, add to or subtract from" any song written. Moreover, the two composers could be loaned out to another studio at any time for a fee paid to Universal, but Loesser and Actman weren't at liberty to accept another job on their own.

Nothing notable came from his association with Universal, and when his contract expired, Loesser moved with Burton Lane's help to Paramount where, beginning with "Man of Manakoora" (music by Alfred Newman) which was sung by Dorothy Lamour in *The Hurricane*, he began his rise to fame in the movies. He composed lyrics for over fifty songs in more than thirty pictures, such as *Destry Rides Again, Happy Go Lucky, Thank Your Lucky Stars, The Perils of Pauline,* and *Let's Dance*. A few of these songs were great successes: "Two Sleepy People" and "Small Fry," both to music by Hoagy Carmichael; "See What the Boys in the Back Room Will Have," music by Frederick Hollander and sung by Marlene Dietrich in *Destry Rides Again*; and "I Don't

Want to Walk Without You, Baby," music by Jule Styne. Loesser's income jumped to five figures, and by 1939 the sign on his office door read "Frank Loe$$er." Two years later, he enjoyed the status of top-flight lyricist in the movie industry.

Cy Feuer, music head at Republic Pictures, arranged for Paramount to loan-out Loesser who was to assist Jule Styne with seven songs in a relatively expensive musical, *Sis Hopkins*. Loesser was less than thrilled at first and he railed at both Republic and Styne. He stormed into Feuer's office, yelling: "You son of a bitch, I'm writing for Hoagy Carmichael now. I'm not coming to work with some half-ass piano player who is really a vocal coach." It took two hours to persuade him to at least talk to Styne who, for his part, attempted to humbly wear his heart on his sleeve: "I've watched horses shimmy in sync. I've written arrangements for coyotes, I've written songs about watermelon and guts and gravy." Loesser paced about the room impatiently, but when he heard Styne's music, he changed his attitude. He did continue to battle Feuer and the film's director, but he and Styne got down to business after posting a sign on their bungalow office: "No Cowboys Allowed, No Horses Allowed, No Gunshots." He and Styne became such good friends that when the war broke out and Loesser left Hollywood for the Army, his parting advice to Styne mixed egotism with pragmatism: "You've been spoiled. There's no one like me....If you want someone like me, don't get a clever rhymer, because there is a rhyming dictionary. Anybody can rhyme, you can find a rhyme for anything. But get a guy who can say something clever and warm, because you need warm lyrics for your music."

Loesser's songs in that pre-World War II period were remarkable for their facility, intelligence, and strength. As Max Wilk remarked, they were not like the usual Hollywood concoctions. Loesser was "on the prowl for a brighter notion, a stronger line. Certainly he could turn out an "I've Got Spurs

That Jingle, Jangle, Jingle'; that was part of the job. For Betty Hutton he could write dynamite material—'Poppa, Don't Preach to Me' and 'He Says Murder, He Says.' And he was already coming up with such gems as 'I"d Like to Get You on a Slow Boat to China.'" But his ballads revealed "the deep strain of romanticism that underpinned his later work." "He really worked from his gut," added Abe Burrows. "He was an incurable romantic"—so much so that Loesser scolded Burrows for wasting his lyric talent on comedy rather than saving it for romance.

The outbreak of the war altered Loesser's career by inspiring him to write music to his own lyrics for the first time. There was a veritable deluge of songs by various composers, and many of these tunes entered popular legend: Jerome Kern's "The Last Time I Saw Paris"; Sammy Cahn and Jule Styne's "I'll Walk Alone"; Nat Burton and Walter Kent's "The White Cliffs of Dover"; Irving Berlin's "White Christmas"; and Irving Kahal and Sammy Fain's "I'll Be Seeing You." Variations on military, patriotic, or homecoming themes were endless, and, as Donald Ewen claims in *Great Men of American Popular Song*: "Everybody who was writing songs was writing about the war."

Loesser's own army songs (particularly "Praise the Lord and Pass the Ammunition" —the first of his war classics— and "What Do You Do In The Infantry?") were highly popular and, like the best of his comic or romantic songs, had bite and strength. "The Ballad of Rodger Young," written to satisfy the infantry's need for a number to glorify its role, became his second war classic. Based on the true story of a heroic private who died while single-handedly attacking a Japanese machine-gun nest on a South Pacific island, the ballad was first heard on Meredith Willson's coast-to-coast radio program in 1945. Its impact was immediate, and the song soon became one of the most frequently sung war tunes and had the distinction of being recorded by Burl Ives, Nelson Eddy, and others.

After the war, Loesser returned to Hollywood and turned out hits such as "Tallahassee," "I Wish I Didn't Love You So" (sung by Dinah Shore), and the Oscar-winning "Baby, It's Cold Outside." Despite these successes, Loesser was dissatisfied with writing for motion pictures.

As he explained in a 1950 interview with Irving Drutman:

> There's no chance for a writer to do anything memorable in musical pictures. Generally, you're given just the three standard situations. The script reads, 'There's a piano in the room. Ethelreda goes over to it and sings.' Then there's the scene where J. Carroll Naish says, 'This little girl here, Betty Grable, is sensational. She'll put our star in the shade. Why don't you give her a chance?' Then we'll pan out to a cabaret, and she sings. And the third situation is where the leading man has told the girl he loves her in an earlier reel and they don't want to repeat, so he sings it to her.

Loesser was also preparing to launch his Broadway career, although nothing came of his countless discussions with John Steinbeck to write oratorios or musical plays, and it was only till *Where's Charley?* in 1948 that he received his first Broadway credit. But the show was slow to catch on, despite praise from Rodgers and Hammerstein, Cole Porter, and other composers. Only when Arthur Schwartz wrote an unsolicited article in the *New York Times*, stating that Loesser was "the greatest undiscovered composer in America," that audiences began to take a solid look at the show.

After this, he struck gold, although he never formally agreed to write *Guys and Dolls*. It was only after Loesser had handed the first four songs to Feuer and Martin that the producers knew they could have a viable show. Loesser didn't actually sign his contract until after the show had opened on Broadway! Although in its final form, *Guys and Dolls* had seventeen numbers, Loesser actually wrote some twenty others that were discarded for various reasons, but mainly because they didn't pass his own standards.

In their piece for *The Guys and Dolls Book*, a commemoration of the 1982 British National Theatre production, Caryl Brahms and Ned Sherrin see a natural link between Runyon and Loesser: "His eccentricities were Runyonesque. He had a phobia about sitting in public places unless his back was to the wall, and the result of teaming him with Runyon was a perfect marriage."

Ernest Martin described how Loesser would rise at around four-thirty or five and make himself a martini to get himself going. He would compose from five to eight before returning to sleep. Then there'd be another three or four hour burst of work, followed by another nap. His time of day was the late night and the wee, wee hours of dawn. Brahms and Sherrin report that it was Loesser who "threw out Swerling's original book; but perversely he still wrote his score around it. However, his sure theatrical instinct developed so rapidly that Burrows found it possible to construct his new story line writing from song to song."

The locales in Act One include Broadway's sidewalks and streets, the Save-a-Soul Mission, the Hot Box, and Cathedral Square in Havana, and this allowed Loesser the freedom to compose in a variety of styles, tones, and tempi. There could not be any fussy or elaborate prelude because Runyon's pace was quick. Runyonland had to be evoked quickly, dazzlingly, and theatrically. It was also important to introduce the underworld milieu and the Salvation Army counter virtually back-to-back, for audiences would need to associate principal characters with specific musical themes. So Loesser structured the first scene in three numbers: one for the important subsidiary characters who would get the show off to a raffish, racy start; one for the contrary moral force; and one to establish Nathan Detroit and his preoccupation with the dice game.

After a brief medley overture, Loesser composed "Fugue For Tinhorns," in which three "bookies" (Nicely-Nicely, Benny Southstreet, and Rusty Charlie) discuss the relative merits of their favoured horses. There was actually no spot in the book for this number, but Loesser insisted: "This *feels* right for me for this property." The producers struggled to place the number somewhere until Martin finally came up with a brainwave: "If you've got no place to put it, why don't you stick it up front, as a genre piece? Where it's not about anything, but it opens the show and sets the whole thing going." The suggestion was perfect. The three horseplayers singing about the morning's selections in racetrack argot set the right notes for the musical's opening. The characters try to outtalk one another: Nicely-Nicely is confident about Paul Revere's chances of winning the race; Benny puts his faith in Valentine's odds; and Charlie boosts his own pick, Epitaph. The comic effect is achieved by what Joseph P. Swain calls the "juxtaposition of musical rightness and dramatic absurdity," for the stanzaic overlapping and repetitions are perfect for the three different opinions on the same subject, while "the musical texture reminiscent of Bach is a typically outrageous translation of the Runyon *personae*."

There is a swift change of mood and tone as the Mission Band enters after the fugue, with tambourine, cornet, bass drum, and cymbals following in the lively wake of the trumpet and horns for the fugue. "Follow the Fold" sounds like (what Goddard Lieberson calls) "a perfectly good Baptist hymn" and is meant to be a rousing injunction against sin, a typical Salvationist exhortation to live by the straight and narrow. Its dramatic function is obvious: it introduces the gamblers' antagonists—the city missionaries from whose company the play obtains the "doll" destined for Sky Masterson. The seriousness of the hymnody (with phrases such as "stray no more," "resist the devil," "the devil's own street," "jungle of sin") emphasizes the traditional puritan force in contention against the licentious denizens of the underworld. The fact that Sarah Brown leads the hymn with sober idealogical conviction sets up the potential for an intense contest between her and Sky. It also lays the groundwork for the comic irony later in her Havana escapade where she repeats the classic formula of a "saint" becoming a "fallen angel."

The ensemble quality of the first act is extended by the third song, "The Oldest Established," which is a profane hymn to Nathan Detroit's floating crap game. That the song was actually composed late in production—during the Philadelphia try-out—does not diminish its genius. It was Abe Burrows who came up with the line about "the oldest established perma-nent floating crap game in New York," prompting Loesser to respond: "That's got a great rhythm to it—let me have it, I have just the tune for it." And so came a Handelian cantata or gamblers' ode—just ten days before the Phildadelphia open-ing—sung by the hoods with serious dignity, hats in hands held over their hearts. Loesser felt it necessary to emphasize that to their way of thinking, the guys weren't loafers. They were in a business: crap-shooting. The oxymoron in the phrase "permanent floating" is very much in the spirit of Runyon's ironic language. A further irony is that this song, "part *alma mater* and part hymn," according to Joseph Swain, comes after the Salvationist hymn and is sung by a brotherhood of crooks with a mixture of college fraternity and quasi-religious fervour. Moreover, it anticipates the prayer meeting in the second act where a rousing gospel number is a show-stopper.

The comic numbers extend to every type of character, from the obviously risible lowlifers and Hot Box girls to even the Salvationists and romantic leads. The Hot Box numbers are, of course, the most overtly comic because of the satire on Miss Adelaide and the very nature of show business. "A Bushel And a Peck" is a parody of the type of loony novelty act performed in nightclubs with burlesque taste. The chorus girls, in abbreviated farm costumes with large hats, rakes, hoes, and pitchforks, say enough in themselves about the low-level titillation and corniness of the number. It's the type of song and lyric that could have been turned out by almost any composer of commonplace wit, and it bears comparison with the seedy nightclub numbers in *Pal Joey* or the vaudeville kitsch in *Gypsy*, though it doesn't strive for the smirking cynicism of *Pal Joey* or the tits-and-ass vulgarity in *Gypsy*. There is an underlying poignancy in the fact that Miss Adelaide, desperate for marriage, sings about loving her man without any evidence of his reciprocation. The tone is one of barnyard drollery, but the placement of the song just before "Adelaide's Lament" points up the comic irony. Originally composed as a "safety," and extensively promoted by Loesser's publisher in advance of the Broadway opening, the song was meant to open the second act but was moved ahead when it became an offstage hit.

"Adelaide's Lament," on the other hand, is ingenious in both style and substance. According to Loesser, the character was originally a striptease whose colds were merely an occupational disease caused by her having to undress in a drafty nightclub. Loesser suggested that her profession be changed to that of singer, arguing that no performer of any stature would really strip in front of a Broadway audience, and if she *did* it might offend the female customers. He also pointed out that if Adelaide's cold were made an infection with an emotional connection to her frustrated love-life with Nathan, the comedy could be carried along for more than just one joke. So, with the psychoanalytic phrases supplied by Burrows, Loesser invented a number that perfectly suggests a woman's trials and tribulations during an inordinately extended engagement to an unreliable gambler:

> The average unmarried female, basically insecure
> Due to some long frustration, may react
> With psychosomatic symptoms, difficult to endure
> Affecting the upper respiratory tract.
> In other words, just from waiting around
> For that plain little band of gold
> A person—can develop a cold.

The song begins with prosaic formality as Adelaide tries to sound dignified, but her nasality undercuts this pretension. The song has a deliberately mixed diction (part stilted sophistication, part vernacular) that suggests the comic tension in her frustrated attempt to sound clinical about an emotional crisis. Loesser's music releases polysyllabic spoken-song into a plaintive, demotic melody with the funny anticlimax. It is a personal song, particularized by Adelaide's frustration, and its comedy is accentuated because the song is delivered by an apparently naive character who is hopelessly awaiting the day she can win her band of gold and fulfill her dream of a Niagara honeymoon and community property. Her fidelity, yearning, and dreaming contrast with Nathan's chronic stalling, and Adelaide's resulting neurosis is a comic peak. As Lehman Engel remarks in *Words With Music*, Loesser's technique enables the audience to experience "something felt as opposed to something observed."

But the song is not pure comedy, despite its witty use of rhyme and situation and its spoof of modern psychoanalysis. There is a tenderness about Adelaide that turns the number into a wry love ballad with a blues flavour. "Adelaide's La-

ment" is character-portrayal, situation comedy, and love ballad all rolled into one. It is the sort of virtuoso piece that
Loesser was convinced could have been written only for the
stage and not the screen. He once described to Irving
Drutman how the number would have suffered in a typical
studio treatment where:

> First we see the door of a doctor's office. Adelaide comes
> out sneezing. She walks down the street, enters another
> door labeled 'Nathan Detroit Enterprises.' His secretary
> says Mr. Detroit isn't in. Adelaide hears dice rattling in
> the inner office, she sneezes again. Next we see her at
> her mother's house. She complains about being engaged
> to Nathan for fourteen years and no marriage, and Mama
> says, 'I've got a cake in the oven, amuse yourself with
> the radio, I'll be right back.' Adelaide turns on the radio
> and 'Dardanella' is playing. That's the song for the
> situation. If you complain to the front office, they say,
> 'What are you kicking about, didn't we establish that
> she's got a cold?'

Unlike his wicked spoof, the number has no extraneous
embellishments. It is the equivalent of a musical soliloquy.
Despite the use of psychological and medical jargon, the language does not seem invented merely for cleverness. Everything fits together, and the wobbling between long, jaw-break-
ing, lung-exhausting lines and more melodic ones is well suited
to a character who is driven into neurosis by her inability to
control her delinquent beloved. In a more primitive context,
she might have contemplated murder.

The theme song follows, and the placement points to an
intentional comic irony, for "Adelaide's Lament" is the flip
side, in a sense, of "Guys and Dolls," which is sung by two
subsidiary characters as a comment on Nathan's attachment to
Adelaide. It was Abe Burrows's idea to use Nicely-Nicely

Johnson and Benny Southstreet as the singers who show that Nathan can be foiled by romance. This sets up a comic dialectic, as it were, between Adelaide's lament and the men's—a point crystallized by the fact that the rhythm, tempo, and style of the title song differ radically from those of Adelaide's tongue-twisting soliloquy. The technique is lively and playful. Loesser doesn't take the easy way out with facile rhyme-scheme ("doll," "small," "tall," "fall," et cetera). Instead, as Goddard Lieberson comments, he shows himself to be either "in a masochistic mood, or in a state of purity," because by taking the position that "doll" has a strict New York pronunciation, he employs it to rhyme with such exotic words as "Taj Mahal" and "Barbasol."

Much more important than this verbal versatility is Loesser's functional purpose. According to the singing duo, romance forces men to sacrifice everything for women: a birthplace, union dues, social freedom, clothing style, and personal luxuries. The refrain "the guy's only doing it for some doll" repeats the complaint, but although the duo have a cynical attitude towards the whole question of romance ("it's too bad that a smart businessman like Nathan has to go and fall in love with his own fiancée"), their song has an upbeat tempo that turns the number into a rousing ribbing rather than a sour roasting.

There is a subtle undercurrent, for the song can also be taken as an oblique comment on Sky Masterson's attraction to Sarah Brown. In this regard, the underlying cynicism (after all, Sky's initial motive in wooing the Mission doll is purely mercenary; he wants to win a bet) yields to romantic power, as a supremely independent male is so transformed that he puts love ahead of gambling, once his true passion. Indeed, it is probably right to conclude that the theme song suits Sky's story better than it does Nathan's, for as Joseph Swain points out, Sky's conversion is implied from the beginning by "his humorous familiarity with the Gideon Bible," whereas there is insufficient motivation for any soul-change in Nathan Detroit.

As Swain phrases it, the show is "a consummate example of the comic love-story formula at its best." That the two pairs of lead characters are fated for the same romantic end is an accepted fact early in the play, despite the apparent obstacles in the path of true happiness. The symmetry of relationships, however, is cleverly varied, for in one case it is the woman (Adelaide) who compulsively pursues the male, while in the other it is the male who begins his pursuit of the female who, it seems, is psychologically and morally opposed to romance. But Loesser's music and lyrics craftily weave a pattern for romance to transcend any obstacle.

As the seminal idea for the musical plot derives from Runyon's tale about Sky and Sarah, it is not surprising to find that the most romantic songs in the first act are distributed between these two characters. Indeed, the distribution is perfectly even, for Sky and Sarah each has a solo by which to express a specific emotion, and their two duets converge toward a common passion.

The pair share a duet at the Mission after Sky, acting on a bet with Nathan, determines to trick Sarah into having dinner with him in Cuba. Actually, Sarah sees right through his cunning charm, but there is no denying that she is also so morally self-righteous that her aversion to sin is also, in part, an aversion to men who are sinners, and therefore to Sky who is one of those sinners. Their confrontation is a prickly one, a moral contest conjoined to the traditional battle of the sexes, and there is utter cunning in the way that Loesser finds the right song to crystallize the conflict and to sum up the characters' varying attitudes to love and life. In themselves, the lines are, perhaps, banal, but in context they make sense for the two characters. Sky and Sarah are from two totally different worlds, so how are they going to get together? Challenged by Sky to describe her type of man, Sarah sounds dogmatically assured, but her description is vague, even though informed by her moral zeal: "I'll know by that calm steady voice/Those two feet on the ground./I'll know, as I run to his arms/That at last I've come home safe and sound." The repetition of "I'll know" legitimates her feeling, though it also subtly betrays her innocence about romance. She is obviously looking for comfort, safety, a haven—all the securities that religion normally offers, at least as propaganda—whereas Sky, who sounds far less certain about his love, sings with utter trust in instinct: "And I'll know long before we speak/I'll know in my heart/I'll know. And I won't ever ask:'Am I right? Am I wise? Am I smart?'" In other words, his love lyric reveals his openness; he is spontaneous, capable of reacting to a given moment without injunctions or prescriptions. On the other hand, Sarah, as he expressly recognizes, has her guy "all figured out" ("You have wished yourself a Scarsdale Galahad/The breakfast-eating Brooks Brothers type"). He will trust his heart to respond to the chemistry of chance.

What is especially interesting musically about the duet is, as Lieberson has remarked, that there is no release or middle theme. The ABC-ABC-A form is very unusual for a popular love-song, but the dramatic moment allows the form to work.

By the end of Sky's lyric, a coda of sorts, Sarah is palpably moved. However, such are the vagaries of the plot that she does not allow herself to burst into romantic expression till much later. Indeed, the first duet ends in a very dramatic, unromantic manner, with her entrancement changing to violence as, reacting to Sky's confident expectation of an embrace, she suddenly hauls off and belts him across the face. The duet works well enough as a love-song abstracted from the play, but the dramatic context sharpens the psychology behind the number and lends added weight to the romantic formula that Loesser is attempting to exploit in words and music.

When Sarah does break out into rapturous romanticism, the song ("If I Were A Bell") is deliciously melodic, free and easy in its feeling and imagery, and spontaneously onomatopoeic. In short, it is everything that would normally contradict her image as a prim and proper spinster, though it is a love ballad that avoids the word "love" entirely. But it works, and with a double twist, both as comedy and as romance. The comedy, in fact, is what fuels the romance, for Sarah is actually drunk when she sings of her rapture. Her tongue loosened by one too many quaffings of *Dulce de Lêche*, her Salvation Army injunctions forgotten, her disgust at Sky's machinations drowned by the sultry sensuality of the Cuban setting, she is a changed woman. The combination of drink and the late night air acts as a potent aphrodisiac, and her heart exults in tipsy lyricism. But all through the song there are flashes of self-recognition on her part, which amplify the comedy of altered chemistry: "Little me with my quiet upbringing/this chemistry lesson I'm learning"; "I knew my morale would crack."

This first full flush of romantic ecstasy leads directly to the next musical sequence for the unlikely pair. Back from Cuba, they stroll down New York's streets. Sky's solo, "My Time Of Day," is a sixteen-bar *arioso*, delivered "slowly and freely" (according to Loesser's prescribed tempo) and with "irregular subdivisions of the beat." Rather than being a dry recitation about the peace and wonder of twilight, it is a tone-poem that reflects its composer's personality as much as its singer's. According to his daughter, Loesser composed this as a love-song to New York city and "the hours that belonged to him, when he would rise at 4:00 A.M. and write, and pace, and smoke, and doodle, and scheme, and contemplate the romance business." Almost as difficult to capture in the listener's ear as to sing because of its quirkily modulating melody, the song is primarily a sequence of images: of the cop, "the janitor with his mop," "the grocery clerks all gone," "the rain-washed pavement," and "the streetlamp light fill[ing] the gutter with gold." The sensuousness turns it into a love song of a city at a specific hour and of the company of a special woman. But the song has another and more important function: it leads, as Joseph P. Swain states, into "the much more stable music and consistent emotion of 'I've Never Been in Love Before.'" In other words, it is a poetic prelude, appropriately short and mood-making, to a romantic setpiece that is really the only explicit love duet for Sky and Sarah.

"I've Never Been in Love Before" brings out the tenderness in both lovers—a tenderness that melts, at least for the moment, the preceding anomalies in each. As Goddard Lieberson has commented, the duet-ballad is made up of only one phrase, "which is diversified through harmonic or slight melodic mutation but always in the same rhythmic pattern." The lovers' tenderness fills their hearts with song, causing the pair to feel helplessly dazed by a strange, strong mutual attraction. And the tenderness possibly accounts for the regular rhythm and the stable underlying harmony. The importance of the lyric is sealed by the fact that it is the concluding song of the first act, although it is necessary to point out that the tenderness is shattered by the clang of a police patrol wagon and the frantic pursuit of the gamblers who bring home to Sarah a sense that she has been deluded by Sky. He is a crafty gambler who wooed her to Havana so that his gambling acquaintances could use the Mission. Consequently, she reverts to her old form of being "a Mission doll" averse to his underworld ways.

The score is poised once again on the horns of romantic dilemma, without quite the overlay of comedy that we find in the case of Adelaide and Nathan. The question is how Loesser will resolve the dilemma without sacrificing the comedy or violating the sense of the music's being integrated with the plot. The answer to this question is one of the least pretentious in Broadway history, although the finale remains open to the objection on grounds of implausibility or, at least, thin probability.

Loesser draws on the idiom and style of the devious but soft characters he had met in the thirties while playing piano at The Back Drop. "Take Back Your Mink," peformed by Adelaide and the Hot Box Girls is a vividly comic number, managing to be an entertaining nightclub satire on the foibles of showgirls as mistresses, though it also has an emotional resonance in the Adelaide-Nathan romance. It sounds like a fresh creation, but it was actually a polished version of a song Loesser used to sing at parties. Technically it is a flat-out presentational number that allows a costume designer, set designer, and chorus girls a brief flash of gorgeous, pseudo-sophisticated satire, and its deft rhythms (how many words, after all, can rhyme with "mink" and not sound phony?) manifest Loesser's virtuosity with comic lyric

> Take back your mink,
> Take back your pearls,
> What made you think
> That I was one of those girls.
> Take back the gown,
> The shoes and the hat,
> I may be down,
> But I'm not flat as all that.

Once again, as in "A Bushel and a Peck" or "Guys and Dolls," the verbal texture is broad "New Yorkese," and much of the fun derives from the chorus girls' Bronx pronunciation of "pearls" and "girls" that clashes with their masquerade of sophistication and the super finery they wear and then discard. But the number is steeped in injured pride, and certainly has a bearing on Adelaide's own emotional dependence on her lying, exploitative fiance. Indeed, the reprise of her lament after this number makes this point eminently clear. But the brave edge to "Take Back Your Mink" is later extended in "Sue Me," a duet with Nathan, in which Adelaide finally loses her temper and (in what Lieberson identifies as a "high-flown Verdian 6/8 rhythm, accompanied by exciting triplets in the brass") accuses Nathan of callous conduct, while he, for the first time, puts by his usual ruses and declares his love for her. The fun is in the clash between her agitation and his desperate calm, though his calm marks a newly-acquired resignation to his fate as her beloved: "Sue me, sue me,/Shoot bullets through me/I love you!" The climax provides the signer with a wonderful opportunity to play the subtext in the song. This is not really a throwaway number (any more than is Eliza Doolittle's "Show Me" sung literally in the face of her foolishly meek Freddie), and Nathan is sincere for a change, though he has to struggle to convince Adelaide of this.

Unfortunately, there is no further development musically of this romantic pairing, and the rest of the show concerns itself with the underworld ambiance and with the Sky-Sarah relationship, with the comedy songs yet again proving to be more vivid and memorable than the softer romantic melodies. But it is not simply showmanship that distinguishes the comedy songs: they are dazzling set-pieces that fit the context and plot, and so they do not seem emptily virtuosic. "Luck Be A Lady," for instance, grows organically out of the sewer crap-game that almost becomes a black farce controlled by Big Jule until Sky overpowers the obnoxious hood and then rolls dice against his fellow-gamblers in a bet to win their attendance at the Save-A-Soul Mission and thus honour his promise to Sarah. For once in his life of outlaw bravado, Sky's gambling has moral stakes. His number to the goddess of the crap game begins as spoken song but the defining melody breaks out and takes over. The song crystallizes a reformation of sorts in Sky, for he is now gambling with a higher motive: he wants to win Sarah's heart and not be dismissed by her as an irredeemable sinner. As such, the song serves as character development and accordingly finds an extra motive for its intensity.

This leaves Arvide Abernathy's sweetly melancholy song in an Irish mode to his granddaughter, Sarah; Nicely-Nicely's show-stopper in the Mission; Adelaide and Sarah's duet; and the finale. Of these, only Nicely-Nicely's "Sit Down, You're Rockin' The Boat" is outside the parameters of romance, though it, too, is integrated with the book. Its gospel styling and zealous enthusiasm fit into the Salvationist theme and support the motif of conversion, although in a robustly comic manner as Nicely-Nicely, supported by a chorus of fellow-crooks, delivers his dream of taking his dice along on a trip to Heaven. The song fits into the plot very well. Sky delivers on his promise to have a throng of sinners show up at the Mission, and the awkward gang are compelled to give testimony to the sins in their hearts; but Sister Sarah impugns Sky's motive, and just when it seems that the meeting is going to fall apart, Nathan prompts Nicely-Nicely into delivering his testimony as a convenient distraction. The stratagem works as all are enveloped by the fervour of the song.

"Sit Down, You're Rockin' The Boat" belongs properly to a discussion of the score's eclecticism. Loesser's interest in romance shows in the double love-plot, though the fairy-tale quality (the show is, after all, subtitled "A Musical Fable of Broadway") allows the artificiality of the stage to inform the romantic conventions. Certainly there is some concession to soft sentimentality in Arvide Abernathy's "More I Cannot Wish You," a sweetly melancholy ballad expressing his wishes for Sarah's happiness, that Goddard Lieberson terms a modal Irish tune. But Sarah is not the sort of character who should be confused with a dewy-eyed, marshmellow-textured ingenue. She is probably the one character who hints at depth in the play, and she has to overcome the palpable disadvantage of serving as a damper to the high spirits of the gamblers. Her heart has to be seen as a real one, something that can be besieged, thrilled, rung, and changed, and Loesser responds to the challenge of creating songs that mark her mutations from oppressive gravity to tipsy hilarity to romantic uncertainty, agitation, and fulfillment.

Sarah is partnered by Adelaide in the canon, "Marry the Man Today," a comical generalization of women's designs on men. Loesser explained to Murray Schumach of the New York Times: "All this says is what every woman is always teaching her daughter: get the man. Marry him. Then worry about him. But you can't do anything with him until you marry him first." The braided lyric—with Adelaide and Sarah's singing a counterpointed duet—is perfect for Adelaide's psychology, because audiences are already too aware of her frustration at being unable to make Nathan take his marriage vows. But how does the song suit Sarah? Well, in this penultimate scene of the play, Sarah is in a haze because she is in love with high-rolling Sky despite her distaste for his notoriety. As the two ladies converse, they share a desire to reform their men. But this is precisely where the comedy of their problematic romances is sharpened. Each woman has a fantasy about love, marriage, and motherhood that is completely unsuited to her prospective mate. So their plan is to marry first, then attempt a conversion of their partners.

The resolution is logical for Sarah and Sky, but is it as such for Adelaide and Nathan? After all, Nathan has already surrendered some of his independence in the comic song, "Sue Me," which shows his being cornered by his fiancée. True, Loesser's score doesn't give him enough musical self-articulation; he is usually evoked by other people's singing about him, as in "The Oldest Established," "Guys and Dolls," and "Adelaide's Lament." Yet, he is ready to change in the face of Adelaide's persistent pursuit, not to mention her fury or chronic humiliation. The crucial question, however, is whether the "Guys and Dolls" reprise at the end is sufficient to bring his romance with Adelaide to its proper, plausible conclusion. Most critics think that it isn't, and they claim that this deficiency is, perhaps, the only flaw in an otherwise superb integration of comedy, romance, and music.

Costume design by Alvin Colt for the character Nathan Detroit.

Mielziner's design, **Guys and Dolls** (1950).

# DESIGNING TRIO

**LOESSER WAS COMMISSIONED** to score *Guys and Dolls* on May 12, 1949, long before the libretto was ever completed. Indeed, the score was in progress long before designers and choreographer were finalized. At first, Jo Mielziner was announced as the set and lighting designer on December 14, 1949, with Jerome Robbins selected on December 26 as choreographer, but Robbins, anticipating an inordinately busy July, declared himself unavailable for the assignment, so Michael Kidd, who had choreographed *Arms and the Girl*, was named as his replacement in April, 1950. Irene Sharaff was expected to do costuming, but she dropped out owing to other commitments, and Alvin Colt, who had designed for Orson Welles and George S. Abbott, was recruited. *Guys and Dolls* was now on course for the next step in the process.

To have Jo Mielziner as designer was a real coup. Born in Paris in 1901, he had received his early education in France. In 1907 he was sent to a boarding school in England and then to New York two years later. He came from cultured stock: his father was a noted portrait painter, his mother a fashion and theatre correspondent for *Vogue*. His ancestors included two prominent nineteenth-century theatre figures, Charlotte Cushman and Dan McGinnis. In 1916, Mielziner was offered a scholarship at the Pennsylvania Academy of Fine Arts, but acting upon the advice of friends and his own parents, he decided to leave school and study painting full time. After brief service in the Marines, he returned to Pennsylvania and in 1920 and 1922 won Cressan Traveling Scholarships, which he used to study contemporary theatre in Europe. His first professional experience came in 1921 when he joined Jessie Bonstelle's stock company in Detroit as actor, designer, and stage manager. He was not keen on being an actor, but his brother Kenneth, a professional who had appeared under the name of Kenneth McKenna, advised him to play small parts in order to see plays from an actor's point of view. So, in 1923 he made his New York début as a bit player and assistant stage manager for the soon-to-be famous Theatre Guild, where he worked under the supervision of Lee Simonson, an expert designer who was very conscious of lighting techniques. Mielziner's career as designer really began in the 1924-5 season when the Guild commisioned him to do Molnar's *The Guardsman* for Alfred Lunt and Lynn Fontanne.

Mielziner made the usual mistakes of a young designer. He mistook means for ends, looked upon the theatre merely as a way of earning a living rather than as a living art, and remained blind to theatre's true values. "I confess my unbounded delight in my early days at seeing my settings revealed by glamorous stage lighting after they were completed at dress-rehearsal time. I almost resented the prospect of actors standing between my picture and the admiring audience!" Despite the revolutionary influence of Robert Edmond Jones, who simplified design to its esentials so that every line counted in terms of theatrical effect, American stage design at this point was still predominantly realistic, sometimes skilfully so, sometimes plainly, tawdrily, or uninterestingly. Mielziner, who first saw Jones' work in 1915, gradually absorbed the master's lessons and discovered that lighting was as important a part of design as décor. He also learned that it was possible to suggest more truth by less explicit detail, at least in the sense of pictorial realism: "The good theatre artist is never 'actual.' He omits the nonessentials, condenses the essentials, accents the details that are the most revealing. He depicts only that part of the truth which he deems necessary to the course of the story."

Mielziner learned avidly from Jones, Simonson, and Joseph Urban, and his own designs became more significant. For The Glass Menagerie (1945), he used translucent and transparent scenic interior walls as a reflection of Tennessee Williams' interest in the inner man. For Finian's Rainbow (1947), he created the atmosphere of a languid, crumbling Southern mansion by painterly effects with translucent aniline on seamless, specially treated muslin. In A Streetcar Named Desire (1947), he made dramatic use of poetic lighting, and the set had a brooding atmosphere even as it resembled an impressionistic X-ray of a New Orleans tenement. Whether he worked in straight dramas or on Broadway musicals, the Mielziner signature was unmistakable: soft and luminous, far from the inspired mannerism of Howard Bay or the expressionism favored by Boris Aronson, and close to the delicate orderliness of Lee Simonson or Oliver Smith.

Feuer and Martin had initially appointed Mielziner to be in charge of direction. This was not surprising for, as Howard Bay admits in his book, Stage Design (1974), there is an ancient adage that "all designers are frustrated directors" because "the process of designing dictates the quasi-director role for the designer. His initial concept must project a schema based on key action patterns. The set is the compass for the journey of the action. " Though the director invariably re-adjusts the compass and even alters the locus of the journey, the designer plots the environment and provides the scope for the show's movement.

On February 7, 1950, Mielziner signed a contract requiring that he "render consultation and supervisory services and make available [his] 'know-how,'" all as would be reasonably required "in the overall production and presentation of the play, including but not limited to script preparation, casting and other pre-rehearsal matters." He was to receive $2,500 in installments of $500, beginning with one upon signing and then $500 each at the end of each week of rehearsal, plus a royalty of 1/2 of 1% of gross weekly receipts. His designing contract was dated March 22, for which he was offered $5,000 in three installments. In a letter to Ernest Martin, dated January 10, 1950, he outlined the definitive start of the design for January 26, with drafting to be completed by February 24. However, the pressure of time forced him to withdraw from the directorial task.

Mielziner's thumbnail sketches, as are usually the custom with preliminaries, were random little imaginings unburdened by practicalities of staging; they were radiations of a dreamer. As the designer's thoughts grew sharper and more definable, so did the sketches, which expressed Mielziner's strong concept of Runyonland.

His designs were a heightened treatment because, as he explained in *Designing for the Theatre*, " a realistic, literal Broadway would look mighty drab and dull as the setting for *Guys and Dolls*, for this wonderful story of Times Square characters [has] vitality, fantasy and the best kind of earthy vulgarity." His Broadway mainstreet was dazzling, but so was his sidestreet off Broadway, with a bright yellow vortex of color set off by purples, blues, and shadows in his color range. This setting was one where Nathan Detroit meets some of his cronies when "looking for action." Mielziner used highlights from neon lettering and signs, and the iconography, appropriately vulgar, absorbed everything from shops, fire-escapes, and poles to cafés and canopies. The Hot Box and dressing room scenes showed nightclub kitsch. One sketch showed blue pipes, a warm pink wall with an orange "No Smoking" sign. In the first rough, the Save-A-Soul Mission was appropriately spartan and drab, with a bastard mixture of chairs to show how the salvationists were dependent on motley donations of furniture. To lend authenticity to his Havana settings, Mielziner obtained six photographs from the Cuban Tourist Commission in New York, two of an Havana lottery, two of the Oriental Race Track, and two of street scenes. While the exteriors at night were bathed in moonlit romanticism, Mielziner based his nightclub drawings on information from the Wendell P. Colton Company that explained how the average Cuban restaurant is open to the street and usually situated on a corner. Mielziner's designs contained such details as white tiled floors, high ceilings with rococo plaster, wooden tables painted black or brown and not fitted with napery, grilles and lattices, lanterns and blinds, and sculpted fighting cocks in silhouette as emblems of one of Havana's gaming pastimes. But the greatest single setting was the underground locale for the crap game, sinuous with cables and steel pipes, colored with blues, pinks, and greens. As the designer himself explained, this was heightened stylization: "No commissioner of Sanitation or Water Commissioner would recognize any of the fanciful pipes or cables in my sewer— transposition of both form and color was essential to keep within the vivid style of this production."

Mielziner's settings were complemented by the color, vibrancy, and raffish comedy of Alvin Colt's costumes. A 6' 7" native of Louisville, Kentucky, where he was born in 1915, Colt received his early theatrical training at the Yale School of Drama. After Yale, in 1937, he arrived in New York with a portfolio of drawings and a letter of introduction to Irene Sharaff who seemed to be having a bad day, because she virtually dismissed him by saying, "Go away and live a happy and peaceful life." But he stayed, and summer theatres in New York State and Rhode Island gave him his first practical experience in stage design. He followed these credits by working for Norris Houghton in Denver and by approaching Lincoln Kirstein in New York. Kirstein had been director for a ballet at the Ogunquit Playhouse, Maine, in 1936, when Colt had worked as electrician. Kirstein advised him to join the designers' union and encouraged him to make new costume sketches. Then Kirstein commissioned him to design for Ballet Caravan's *Charade*, in which Colt used a lace curtain to get an old-fashioned look for the leading lady's costume. After success in this, Colt found himself working on other ballets, which led to his Broadway début in *On The Town*. This was impressive enough, but the young designer demonstrated his versatility and energy with particular force in *Music In My Heart* (1947), creating sets and two hundred costumes that incorporated such textures as ermine, Persian lamb, white fox, and mink.

Colt's penchant was for color and odd materials. He was known to have transformed twenty silk parachutes into billowing skirts by adding waistbands and ruffles. Once, as Dorothy Barret reported in *Dance*, he got Madame Karinska, one of his mentors, to crochet circles by hand in order to obtain the effect of dotted material. Colt was candid about his debt to her and to Russian painter Pavel Tchelitchew for an understanding of art. "Color is the most important element to consider on stage," Colt once remarked, "and color relates directly to the subject matter." A smoky cabaret scene, for instance, calls for smoky colors; a Mexican scene, for hot, arid colors. But he was quick to add that in order to be effective on stage, colors should not be familiar to the eye. For example, "shocking pink" did not seem at all striking on stage at the time it was supposed to be a fashion favorite.

*Guys and Dolls* provided Colt with an especial challenge in that the costumes were supposed to be comic without necessarily being caricatural, and tacky without being distractingly ugly. Colt read a lot of Runyon stories first in order to get the flavor and character, then stood and looked at people outside Lindy's. His costume bible for the males included green-and-white squares or stripes of all colors, including orange and purple. These suits were purchased on Orchard Street, and the stripes were embroidered on by Brooks Costume. The shirts also had a range of bold colors—the only white ones were worn by the detective—and were bought by him from Benhill haberdashers on Broadway or made to specification by Nat Lewis. The ties, of colorful satin, came mostly from Tie City, also on Broadway, although the hats (whose colors included oranges, greens, and blues) were purchased in Philadelphia during the show's tryout. "Aren't they terrible?" he laughed. "All the wrong kind of tailoring! The worst! Positively the worst!"

So successful was Colt in his costuming that critic John Mason Brown, who had never counted himself a Runyon admirer, found himself relishing this "fable of Broadway." Recognizing that Runyon's world was "a special world within a special world," with a distinct fairy-tale quality, Brown thought the costumes, especially of the "dice-artists," were "fabulous." "They are such suits as Broadway itself has never seen except in nightmares. Their colors are violent, their stripes wide as bridle paths, their vests cut as low as evening gowns."

Colt alarmed many a salesgirl on Broadway when he shopped around for black girdles for his "dolls." The designer went for shocking effects. His Adelaide would dress in blue for "Sue Me," yet carry a pink purse, while Nathan would wear dark gray pinstripes, pink tie, and carnation. For the corny "A Bushel and A Peck" number, Colt didn't think that ordinary gingham was showy enough, so he used a special hand-screened print. The girls' skirts were a nightclub version of an apron, more like southends of Bikini bathing-suits. Their bras were a pair of daisies, whose petals the girls pulled off one by one when mouthing "He loves me; he loves me not."

Whereas the Mission ladies were generally patterned to the straight and narrow in silhouette and texture in maroon and gray—although they were permitted blue ribbons, with Sarah eventually given a ruffled collar after Isabel Bigley had wept for not having any beautiful costumes with which to enchant a dear girlfriend from schooldays—the Hot Box girls revelled in vulgarity. The brassiest touch, however, developed late in production—during the Philadelphia tryout, as a matter of fact, when "Take Back Your Mink" was newly installed in the show, forcing Colt to rush a furrier down from New York to make "mink" stoles from mink-dyed marmot. Lingerie was obtained from ready-to-wear stores, but because it was thought too suggestive to have sheer black chiffon, appliquéd with fig leaves and hands, Colt used black elastic panty girdles. He removed the supporters and arranged a decoration of blue ribbons.

No showgirl or leading lady would dare question Colt's choices with impunity, for if she didn't think her waistline was right, for example, Colt would pull himself up to his full formidable height and drawl in his Louisville manner: "Honey, you don't think I'd let you wear anything you don't look right in, do you?"

Moreover, with Michael Kidd in charge of choreography and movement, there was little chance that any of the cast would fail to look right in the superbly designed environment. A gnomish native of Brooklyn (born in 1919), Kidd had majored in chemical engineering at City College but had grown bored with the field. "No laughs, no people, too lonely." He enrolled in dance school, although it was not easy at the time for a young male from Brooklyn to pull that off: "My folks thought I was crazy and were ashamed to tell the relatives." He studied ballet with Vilzak-Schollar and Muriel Stuart, danced with the Metropolitan Opera Ballet, and came under the influence of Lincoln Kirstein at the School of American

Ballet. His first dancing part on Broadway was in Max Reinhardt's Jewish musical epic, *The Eternal Road*, in 1937, when Kidd was not yet out of his teens. This project had a text by Franz Werfl (author of *The Pure in Heart, Juarez and Maximilian*, and, much later, *The Song of Bernadette*) and the backing of Meyer Weisgal, a passionate Zionist who had channelled his money and convictions into various theatrical spectacles. It also had Lotte Lenya and Kurt Weill. Although Kidd could hardly compete against the lavish spectacle, he did well enough and received further assignments for American Ballet, Ballet Caravan, and Ballet Theatre.

One of his most remarkable projects was for Ballet Theatre in 1942 when he revived Aaron Copland's *Billy the Kid*, in which he danced the title role. Edwin Denby thought his performance showed "verve and a sinister elasticity," and it became clear that Kidd could have as American a style as Jerome Robbins had. As George Amberg put it in *Ballet: The Emergence of an American Art*, Kidd had "the same directness and sincerity [as Robbins], the same natural and relaxed sense of humor, the same keen intelligence and gift of observation, the same friendly and affectionate trade with his fellows," but Kidd possessed "a sharper edge and more comment in his characterizations."

He also created *On Stage!* for Ballet Theatre, a sweetly humorous backstage story about a stagehand and a frightened auditioner. Denby adjudged Kidd's "first big-time work as a choreographer" to be "lowbrow in sentiment, ambitious in size," and rather unsubtle as dance invention. George Amberg, however, praised Kidd's choreography for its departure from the essential foundation of classical ballet, and drew attention to the amount of "unballetic material, of straight acting and incidental speech." It was clear that Kidd was ready to try anther form of dance, and the proof came in Finian's Rainbow (1947), which drew great praise, especially from Brooks Atkinson who wrote in The New York Times:

> If the American musical stage continues to improve, it will no longer be necessary for anyone to speak dialogue on the stage. Everything essential can be said in song and dancing [sic]. Against a wide and rhapsodic setting by Jo Mielziner, the ballet dancers of 'Finian's Rainbow' begin the evening with some lyrical springtime rites of real glory. If notes of music could leap across the stage, they would be no lighter or livelier than this joyous ballet of a young and free people....Mr. Kidd and his band of dancers have interpreted the theme of 'Finian's Rainbow' like thoroughbreds and artists.

In this show, as Amberg pointed out, Kidd used dance extensively, even to the extent of supplying a mute girl (performed by a young Anita Alvarez) with a leading part "entirely and delightfully conceived in pure dance terms." Amberg concluded that Finian's Rainbow was not only a more mature work than On Stage!, but "in absolute terms of value a theatre piece of responsibility, integrity and impeccable style."

Wishing for a more rounded career than he could have had simply in ballet, Kidd was only too happy to turn to musical theatre. His versatility enabled him to show various phrases, idioms, and style to great effect: tap, jazz, acrobatics, burlesque. He could choreograph straight ballet and modern interpretive, as well as parody the forms. Wit and exuberance marked his best work, even in such things as cartwheels, somersaults, backflips, handstands, splits, and bold leaps.

For Guys and Dolls, Feuer and Martin left most of the selection of the dancers to Kidd. Their only instruction concerned the ladies: "Make them the best-looking dancers on Broadway. Honeys with a Ziegfeld kind of zing about them." The most ravishing beauties of the 300 applicants came from outside New York. Two were Canadian: Barbara Ferguson, a twenty-five year old brunette from Toronto, and Onna White, a twenty-six year old taffy blonde from Powell River, British Columbia, who would eventually become one of Broadway's most celebrated choreographers. Both young ladies were featured in "A Bushel and a Peck," a deliberately corny number sung offkey and danced flat-footed by an ensemble of tired showgirls.

The male contingent was drawn from dancers with strong character, but there were some very unlikely candidates. Ernest Martin reported that seventy tramps would show up for the daily tryouts, looking "as though they had just crept out from under rocks" and claiming that they were the originals on whom Runyon had patterned his characters. Kidd's final choices added up to interesting adult delinquents, rich in startling types and gusty, gaudy, uproarious in their movements. Indeed, story and movement were so "closely interwoven," remarked John McClain later, "as to be barely discernible as separate entities. This compelled the choreographer to work in close collaboration with the authors as well as the composer." The success of this was revealed in the prologue performed through dance, movement, and pantomime, and where the scene was set for the story to follow.

Kidd's work on Guys and Dolls followed in the tradition of dance directors rather than in that of director-choreographers. It was a robust hybrid of precision and freedom, especially for the prologue and underground crap game. The idiom was distinctly American and pulled out all the stops when required. However, the choreography did not direct the dialogue or story—the way Jerome Robbins' was to do in West Side Story and Fiddler on the Roof—and as the show was not conceived or directed by Kidd, the choreographer's concepts of dance did not dictate the overall form of the production.

The crap game sequence treated audiences to kinetic excitement that escalated with every backflip, split, and high leap, and, though in one sense it was a setpiece, it was dramatically indicative of the musical's emotional content. The dancing had impact: though carefully conceived for timing and cumulative effect, it was never cold as it explored the scope of the situation, characters, and mood with authentic flair. The dancers became daring denizens of a blowsy underground, defining the suspense and danger of the scene while making vigorous use of the physical space whose stylized décor by Jo Mielziner (the tangle of pipes and the big, sweeping curve of a broad tube) promoted immediate acceptance of the "unreality." Indeed, the choreography aspired to an artistry based on interpretation through expressive movement.

Kidd's work contracted and expanded in colour, shape, and mood, and its translations of diverse experiences (such as Broadway sightseeing, hucksterism, gambling, nightclub burlesque, romantic complaint and agitation, et cetera) focussed attention on the text and characters. The Kidd idiom had an urban look, for virtually everything was earthbound. Even when movement grew airborne—as in moments of the crap game—the exhibitionism had sociological point in its vernacular vocabulary. The sewer background acquired a strange, hitherto unsuspected glamour.

Kidd's choreography incarnated the Times Square milieu, where the tensions, suspicions and feuds, the petty disasters and triumphs, the gaudy romances and comedic follies of its inhabitants seemed to be a thoroughly true record of Broadway society of that era. Jo Mielziner's décor and lighting, Alvin Colt's costuming, and Kidd's choreography were all in perfect harmony in a microcosm of the glitteringly raffish, a Runyonland democracy of hucksters, its characters and caricatures self-absorbed within their own neighbourhood. Without being in the least pretentious, the designing trio made artistic integration a seal of this musical, turning "integration" into a catchword for musical theatre.

# KAUFMAN

**FEUER AND MARTIN** both wanted George S. Kaufman to direct, but he always seemed to have a full schedule and was on an European honeymoon in the summer of 1950, having married his second wife, the actress Leueen MacGrath. The producers did not want to engage in long distance negotiation with him, especially as they had heard that Kaufman was not particularly interested in musicals, and certainly not one produced by men about whom he knew very little. But the producers and Frank Loesser wanted him because his extraordinary credits as playwright and director had stamped him "a past master of show business," one who had "learned every trick of the trade and invented many a new one." Walter Kerr praised his "essentially analytical mind" and beautiful craftsmanship. Howard Taubman thought him "a hell of a writer" with a "sense of professionalism in every play in which he was involved." Richard Watts claimed that Kaufman "brought to the theatre a tremendous vitality and inspired a brightness in other people." Kaufman had the greatest track record in the American theater, starting in 1918 and continuing to the present. Not even a notoriously publicised affair with Mary Astor, which began in 1934 and which brought attention to his sexual skills, deflected respect for his theatrical acumen.

Born in Pittsburgh, Pennsylvania, in 1889, he studied law briefly before trying his hand at business, typing, stenography, sales, and even acting before turning to journalism once he moved to New Jersey. His first big newspaper break came when Franklin P. Adams (FPA) accepted his contributions to a column called "Always In Good Humor" in the *Mail*. Kaufman joined a distinguished group of contributors that included Sinclair Lewis, Edna St. Vincent Millay, Deems Taylor, Dorothy Parker, Alexander Woollcott, Edna Ferber, and Ring Lardner. As his contributions increased, so did his popularity with FPA who invited him to lunch, marking the start of a solid friendship. When the Washington *Times* sought a young writer for a humor column in 1912, FPA recommended Kaufman who was hired at $20 a week for six columns a week. Kaufman moved to Washington and undertook his first column, "This and That and a Little of the Other," which first appeared on December 9. Gauging the wide popularity of the writing, his editor asked him to write seven columns a week and raised his salary to $25 a week. Kaufman's column received wide attention across the country, with many newspapers running excerpts. But his swift success was cut short abruptly by an office accident when he bumped into his publisher, knocking him to the floor. His boss, who had had a very bad day and who had never personally met Kaufman, looked up at him in outrage, rose slowly, and asked: "Who is that Jew in my composing room?" Kaufman was summarily dismissed. He never forgave this anti-Semitism.

When his father moved the family to New York City, Kaufman joined them. He was fortunate to have FPA's help again, landing the job of drama reporter on the *Tribune*. His new boss was Heywood Broun, the celebrated columnist, who assigned him to interview performers and producers in addition to writing reviews of plays and variety shows. After a year of this work—during which time he also studied Dramatic Composition under Harvey Hatcher Hughes at Columbia University—Kaufman became a columnist for the *Mail* with "Be That as It May" in 1915. He received heavy fan mail, but once again, success was short-lived: the paper was sold, and Kaufman returned, with FPA's help, to the drama department of the Tribune, though he continued to sell freelance magazine pieces. Kaufman rose to the rank of drama editor. His own experience at playwriting began with a one-act farce, Going Up, which caught the interest of Henry R. Stern, son of the owner of Burns and Mantle, who was then a play-reader for a major publisher and who ranked Kaufman first on a list of promising playwrights. Yet, despite rewriting Going Up fifty-five times, Kaufman was unable to sell the work and, marking it down as a failure, tossed it into a desk drawer. What Kaufman did not know at the time was that the play had caught the eye of John Peter Toohey, chief play-reader for George C. Tyler, who passed it along to Tyler. The producer, who had introduced New York to George Arliss, George Bernard Shaw, Sarah Bernhardt, the Abbey Players, Mrs. Pat Campbell, John Barrymore, and Jeanne Eagels, remembered the young playwright when Among Those Present, a melodramatic comedy, got into trouble and needed a radical re-write. Kaufman was invited to do the revision, which he did expeditiously, working in a funny character called Dulcinea (Dulcy, for short), who had been created by Franklin P. Adams and frequently quoted in Adams' column. Kaufman secretly intended the role for Lynn Fontanne, and after the play had opened to some success, he set about writing a second version with a new title, Someone in the House, to star Fontanne. Unfortunately, the production lasted less than five weeks on Broadway, prompting Kaufman to crack to Tyler: "Let's change the title to No One in the House."

Kaufman's wit became justly celebrated. A tall, thin man with a perpetual slouch, he had a big, thick nose, unruly hair, and inelegant eyeglasses. Although he was shy in many social situations, he had a sharp mind, brilliant articulation, and a devastating satiric sense. He detested waiters and cab-drivers, and often demolished them with ironic epigrams, but his wit was just as deadly on salesmen and movie moguls. When a salesman tried to sell him stock in a gold mine by claiming that the gold was simply on the ground for the taking, Kaufman feigned disgust: "On the ground? You mean I'd have to stoop for it? Not interested!" When Adolph Zukor, head of Paramount, wired him: "Offer thirty thousand for *Dinner At Eight*," Kaufman wired back: "Offer forty thousand for Paramount." His play on words was often classic—as in the pun "One man's Mede is another man's Persian" or as in his droll comment on a college girl who eloped: "She put the heart before the course."

Such wit more than equipped him to join the Algonquin Round Table which began a fad of celebrity-studded restaurants: Vincent Sardi's (dominated by theatre folk), the Colony (frequented by the Social Register group), and Toots Shor (filled with athletes). But the Algonquin circle was in a class by itself, for its members lived passionately and by their massive egos and wits. Their poker contingent called itself The Thanatopsis Literary and Inside Straight Club. During a game, Kaufman said: "I'd like to have a review of the bidding, with the original inflections."

Even though he had enviable competition from Dorothy Parker, Heywood Broun, Alexander Woollcott, Ring Lardner, and Marc Connelly, Kaufman made his wit sing as it cut. He once said to Howard Dietz, author of *Between the Devil*, "I understand your new play is full of single entendre." When Moss Hart proposed adapting the novel *Gentlemen's Agreement* into a film, he asked Kaufman for his opinion and was told: "I don't have to pay three fifty to find out what it feels like to be a Jew." And he could be tough on actresses. Ruth Gordon once went to some lengths to describe the new play in which she was appearing: "There's no scenery at all. In the first scene, I'm on the left side of the stage and the audience has to imagine I'm in a crowded restaurant. In Scene Two, I run over to the right side of the stage and the audience has to imagine I'm home in

my own drawing room." After listening politely, Kaufman retorted: "And the second night, you'll have to imagine there's
an audience out front."

His penetrating intelligence turned him into a "play doctor" who shuttled between New York, New Haven, Boston,
Philadelphia, Atlantic City, and Washington, D.C. He was val-
ued for his ability to supply a badly-needed line or an idea for
a curtain or a funny bit of business or an excellent cut. But his
greatest value was his ability to dig the best out of people
with whom he was working.

As a playwright and director, his name was synonymous
with quality. His hits included *Beggar on Horseback*, *The Butter and
Egg Man*, *The Cocoanuts*, *The Royal Family*, *Animal Crackers*, *Strike Up The
Band*, *Once In a Lifetime*, *The Band Wagon*, *Of Thee I Sing*, *Dinner At Eight*, *You
Can't Take It With You*, *The Man Who Came To Dinner*, *The Front Page*, *The Late
George Apley*, *Of Mice and Men*, *My Sister Eileen*, and *Over Twenty-One*.
Many of his successes were collaborations with Marc Connelly,
Edna Ferber (described by Woollcott as "a mixture of Little
Nell and Lady Macbeth"), Herman J. Mankiewicz, Morrie
Ryskind, Ring Lardner, Alexander Woollcott, Moss Hart,
Howard Dietz, and John P. Marquand. This penchant for col-
laboration earned him some grudging admiration from critics who carped that he really couldn't write a successful play
on his own. Walter Kerr explained that Kaufman "had essentially an analytical mind. The person who collaborates tends to
be a craftsman, constructionist, analyst, critic, what have you.
It seems to me that he did extraordinarily well, that he was a
beautiful craftsman, that his greatest strength as a playwright
was his wit."

George Oppenheimer concurrred: "He was responsible
for marrying very high farce and very high comedy, and with
his wit, it came out satire." Kaufman's professionalism distinguished every play and, as Howard Taubman asserted, his sat-

ire was "sharp, keen edged. It wasn't bloody. His whole cast of mind was saturnine and sardonic, and directed that way, it did wonderful things in the theatre."

His productions had a special touch, no matter how earnestly he sought to keep his directorial hand in the background. Max Gordon commented: "There was a neat, unified pace to those plays. The comedy always seemed sharper and wittier under his guidance. The lines and situations seemed always to have been heightened by his unnerving eye and ear."

As he directed, he would sit quietly in the third or fourth row, with eyes closed or half-closed, and chin cradled in the palm of a hand. He would sometimes chew on candy bars or chocolate or fudge, and he rarely spoke or interrupted while a scene was in progress, but after uncurling his long legs, he would stand up, and summon an actor or author to a quiet corner to explain why something wasn't right.

Of course, when occasion demanded, he would resort to deadly wit to make his point, but such occasions were rare and completely justified his irony. Irritated one evening to find his actors misbehaving on stage, he sent the cast a telegram: "I WAS HERE TONIGHT. WHERE WERE YOU?" In another instance, he sent a note: "11 A.M. REHEARSAL TOMORROW TO REVOKE ALL IMPROVEMENTS TO THE PLAY PUT IN SINCE THE LAST REHEARSAL." Even the irrepressible Marx Brothers once felt his sting. Given to outrageous ad-libbing during The Cocoanuts, they clowned to the point of callous disregard for the text. Kaufman, who was watching a rehearsal while chatting to Heywood Broun, suddenly cut off the conversation, walked close to the stage and listened, and then returned to explain to an annoyed Broun: "I thought I heard one of the original lines of the show." Despite his enormous prestige as playwright and director, Kaufman never took success for granted. He worried incessantly about becoming a failure and consequently earned the nickname of "the gloomy dean of Broadway." Yet, he wasn't gloomy in the presence of a cast. As Saint Subber once recalled: "There was a relaxed blue-room quality about his rehearsals: all right, ladies and gentlemen, now it's time for work. And they would work. Now it's time for play, and there would be laughs, lots of laughs."

Kaufman had a modest opinion of himself and the nature of stage direction, as he showed in a note he wrote for John Gassner's *Producing the Play*: "My own opinion—and I hope it will go no further or I shall certainly lose out on some jobs— is that the whole business of direction is overrated....Personally, I am always a little suspicious when the director is too highly praised. A play is supposed to simulate life, and the best direction is that which is so effortless and natural that it simply isn't noticed at all." When Lynn Fontanne telephoned to ask him if a certain young man was a good director, he responded: "He's a good director when he has a good play. When he has a bad play, he's a bad director."

Kaufman did have one remarkable quirk: a distinct antipathy to the Broadway musical. During the production of *Animal Crackers* (1928), starring the zany Marx brothers, Kaufman had not seemed to care about the music. As recalled by composer Harry Ruby: "Once, when I played him a conceited number from the show that ran about ten minutes, all he said was: 'Peppy!'" Howard Teichmann claimed that Kaufman "had no knowledge and very little understanding of song writing. 'Let's have a walk,' he'd say. 'That's a song title. It's that easy. 'Sit down on a bench.' That's a song title, too. 'Time to go home.' Another song title. 'Let's have a cup of coffee.' A fourth song title. 'Pass me the cream, my dear.' What a ballad!" Teichmann was of the opinion that Kaufman's attitude "was that of a postman toward a heavy mailbag: odious but necessary."

Kaufman's ignorance about music affected his professional judgment adversely, perhaps never more glaringly than when he failed to recognize the potential of Irving Berlin's "Always," which the composer had written specially for *The Cocoanuts*. Berlin himself was fond of telling the story of a friend who met Kaufman on the street one day while the director was at work on an adaptation of Gilbert and Sullivan. The friend inquired: "How's it going, George?" "Great!" Kaufman replied. "It's wonderful working with a dead composer."

But while Kaufman had some familiarity with show music, he didn't with Damon Runyon. After he signed (in July, 1950) to direct, he was sent from Ernest Martin three scenes and the plot outline. The director admitted: "I've never read a single Runyon story in my life." "Then it's time you began your education," Martin retorted. But Kaufman was reluctant to take on *Guys and Dolls*. He had heard that Feuer and Martin had been difficult to work with during *Where's Charley?* However, Martin prevailed upon him to read the beginnings of Burrows' script, after which Kaufman shook his head and said, "Abe can get closer to the flavor of Broadway than that. Abe has the talent to make the material a lot funnier." But Frank Loesser cautioned: "Not *too* funny." Burrows knew that Kaufman was right. "My dialogue was not as funny as I could make it. I was being overly cautious. All this because it was the first time I was writing for Broadway and I was worried about people like Brooks Atkinson, Richard Watts, John Chapman, and their scary critical colleagues." In an interview with Howard Teichmann, he related:

> I had a rule with Kaufman. I told my wife,'Look, this is my first show. I'm going to do exactly everthing this man tells me because this guy does the kind of theatre I understand.' And I did. From the moment he started the show, I did exactly what he told me to do. He and I never had a single argument in connection with the show.

The only disagreement was over the question of tenderness on stage. Kaufman loathed love scenes of any kind, but knowing that Burrows felt a tenderness for the raucous guys and gunmen and gamblers, he finally made a concession. However, if Kaufman wanted a particular cut, Burrows would swiftly comply. Sometimes, if Kaufman cut a  little deeply to test a particular moment, he would acknowledge, "Perhaps we cut a bit too deeply, Abe." Then the cut lines would be restored.

After Burrows had finished most of the first draft, Kaufman invited him to his home in Bucks County. Burrows had no idea what was in store for him. He was forced to work in a little room where Kaufman kept all his awards, including the Pulitzer Prize. The room was under the eaves and became hot. No matter. Burrows was expected to keep focussed, despite the merry conversation of guests on the terrace and right through the maid's invitation to lunch. Without consulting Burrows, Kaufman imperiously announced, "Abe, will have lunch in his room."

Kaufman would never let him get away with anything. When a joke was repeated twice in the script, Kaufman remarked: "Abe, you've done that same joke three times." Burrows protested: "George, we often do that on radio. We call it a running gag." Kaufman would have none of this: "Abe, radio is free. The people coming to see your show have to buy tickets. Give them a new joke."

For his part, Kaufman grew to admire Burrows' facility in coming up with the right answer to troublesome questions. One such moment was just before the first-act curtain, where Vivian Blaine as Miss Adelaide was draped in pots and pans at a kitchen shower given by her Hot Box girlfriends. Feeling that a new laugh was desperately needed in this situation, Kaufman turned to Burrows during a rehearsal and said: "Abe, we've got to have one of your howitzers here—one of your big ones."

After a moment's meditation, Burrows suggested that a drunk stagger on stage, stare at Adelaide's accessories, and blurt out: "What vulgar jewelry!"

Burrows found Kaufman's barbs "painful at times," though one of the things that hurt the most was a quiet "Oh, dear." Thinking that a freshly rewritten scene was quite good, Burrows was shaken when Kaufman looked at it and sighed softly, "Oh, dear." Just that—"Oh, dear"—which could mean several things: the scene was clumsy or the language was flowery or the mood was too tenderly romantic for Kaufman's liking. When it came to love scenes, Burrows distrusted Kaufman who had a tendency to shy away from romance on the stage even though he had done many shows full of beautiful and tender moments.

On the matter of construction, however, Kaufman was undisputed master. Burrows realized that a playwright was "a man who constructs a play," and as he added in his memoir: "He is like a wheelwright, or a shipwright, or any other wright who is, as Webster says, 'a constructive workman; an artificer; one who is engaged in a mechanical or manufacturing business.'" Burrows took Webster to heart, knowing full well that a playwright's good story and snappy dialogue could be "smothered by a jumble of badly placed bricks" if his construction was faulty. So he put his faith in Kaufman who treated him as "a member of the Bricklayers' Union."

The beginning of a play is crucial to engaging an audience. Neither Kaufman nor Burrows wanted a "feather duster" opening, with the usual maid busily dusting the usual furniture and providing expository information on the phone to the usual invisible caller. Burrows tried to have a funny opening, burying the plot in comic business in an almost frantic attempt to grab the audience's attention. But Kaufman reminded him that theatre was not like television: there was no need to assume that the audience's attention-span was going to be so short as to require speedy diversion. "They've paid good money to see your work and they'll be patient with you at the beginning of the show. They are not going to get up and leave and there are no knobs to turn. So take a deep breath and set up your story."

Kaufman was a brilliant teacher, but he was "no kindly Mr. Chips." Whenever Burrows rang his apartment doorbell for their meetings, Kaufman, who was not very big on greetings or farewells, would nod cursorily and wait until Burrows had wiped his feet on the doormat before admitting him inside. Kaufman insisted on punctuality, which was fine with Burrows who had been disciplined by uncompromising radio and television schedules. However, because of his heavy load of television work on the side, Burrows was sometimes a little late for their meetings, much to Kaufman's dislike. Kaufman would grumble quietly, then glower at Burrows. When the latter once tried to neutralize Kaufman's displeasure by quoting Oscar Wilde's epigram, "Punctuality is the thief of time," Kaufman responded in a chilly voice that he thought it a witty line but not funny.

When *Guys and Dolls* was close to rehearsals, Burrows was guided through every line by Kaufman for a final polish. The director expected total concentration and would brook no distraction. Burrows earned Kaufman's wrath one time after he was invited to a *bar mitzvah* for columnist Leonard Lyons' eldest son. The solemn ceremony got off to a fair start, but the rabbi, impressed by celebrities in attendance (people such as Bernard Baruch, Rodgers and Hammerstein, Leland Hayward, Billy Rose, Ferenc Molnar, et cetera), seized the opportunity to wax eloquent. The ceremony turned into an epic of prolonged oration—prompting Molnar's remark: "Abe, this is a very long rabbi"—and Burrows was hours late for his meeting with Kaufman who turned livid with anger. "You're an amateur!" he fumed. "You're wasting your strength on a lot of nonsense."

Once his fury was spent, he said, "Let's get on with this damn thing"—his curt way of acknowledging affection for Burrows' libretto.

Discipline was a religious credo in Kaufman's theatre work. Anything that diminished it was sinful. Trouble was that Kaufman had his strong biases and was not effusive in his praise. He examined every detail with a dry, sour sense of humour. Once he had made up his mind about something, it was almost impossible to get him to change it.

Michael Kidd, for instance, had given considerable thought to staging the crap game as a dance. But Kaufman was not very agreeable to the idea. "Mike, I don't understand. How are you going to have a scene where these tough gamblers will be standing around the stage while a bunch of dancers get up and do a dance?"

Kidd countered: "I'll incorporate all the members of the cast into the crap game. I'll have Nathan taking a cut of every pot, I'll have Big Julie rolling. I'll have all the different characters participate."

"Well, I can't see it. It beats me."

Kidd, however, persisted, and after working out his choreography and demonstrating it to everybody, in the full knowledge that Kaufman was dead set against it, he presented the number in rehearsal. Kaufman showed no sign of emotion. At the conclusion, he turned to Kidd and said: "Mike, I hardly have to tell you you've done something very remarkable here. Okay, let's go on."

That sort of compliment, though quickly passed off, was far better than nothing, and was the biggest accolade one could get from the director.

No one defied Kaufman—or if one did, it wasn't for long.

Frank Loesser once had an exchange of words with him over reprises of songs in the second act. Their voices grew higher with each serve and volley, until Kaufman suddenly stood up quietly and said rather menacingly: "I'll tell you what, Frank. I'll let you reprise as many songs as you want in the second act if you let me reprise some of the jokes from the first act."

Game, set, and match to Kaufman.

Of course, Kaufman insisted on treating *Guys and Dolls* as a play interrupted by musical numbers. Indeed, he regarded the songs as "lobby" numbers in the sense that every time a song started, he sprinted for the lobby. During one of these sprints, Abe Burrows overheard him muttering, "Good God, do we have to do every number this son-of-a-bitch ever wrote?"

Frank Loesser (1910-1969)

# "SHE WON'T TALK TO ME
# SINCE I HIT HER "

**FRANK LOESSER** was very involved in casting the show. His daughter's memoir informs us that at the time, "one of his techniques for determining a singer's range was to have him or her sing 'Blue Skies' over and over, higher and higher, louder and louder." Auditioning male singers were expected to "sing a hot 'Blue Skies,' look like bums, and talk like gangsters," while aspiring Hot Box girls "had to screech their lyrics in a parody of a cheap chorus line and, at the same time, make sure every word was clear." And this was not all: singers were also required to demonstrate their lung-power by yelling. "Yell for help," Loesser would order. "Loud." Actors' Equity was bombarded by reports about the weirdness of auditions. But there was a reason to the apparent madness. Broadway had not yet introduced "miking" for musicals, and even when that technology did arrive, Loesser wanted no part of it. He demanded that a voice should be heard distinctly and easily from the rear balcony. Years later, during rehearsals for *The Most Happy Fella*, his musical version of Sidney Howard's *They Knew What They Wanted*, "Loud Is Good" became his dictum. This slogan was posted in prominent places so that none of the cast could miss the message. The motto was really an injunction.

Casting for the show was managed to a large extent by Martin Baum and Abe Newman, both of whom were really neophyte theatrical agents. The two approached Feuer and

Martin and said: "You're two guys just starting out in the producing business, and we're two guys just starting out in the
agent business. Give us the nod and we'll become your casting
agents." Equity rules at the time granted freedom to raid other
agents' clients, which the two did most enterprisingly.

Kaufman, however, was not wholly pleased with his cast.
At every audition, seventy tramps showed up, claiming to be
the originals on whom Runyon had patterned his characters.
"If you ask me," commented Martin, "they look as though
they had just crept out from under rocks."

A professional to his finger-tips, Kaufman expected utter
professionalism from his ensemble, but for *Guys and Dolls* he
had a mixed bag of seasoned veterans, newcomers who had
more enthusiasm than craft, and performers who, for all their
undeniable talent, were playing against type. On the positive
side, there was Netta Packer (General Matilda B. Cartwright)
who had been on stage since the age of three and who had
sung in vaudeville before making her legitimate debut at six-
teen. Paul Reed (Lt. Brannigan), with his slow-burn explo-
siveness, was another veteran, though of musicals rather than
of straight plays. Tom Pedi (Harry the Horse), a native New
Yorker, had débuted as Mussolini in the 1937 revue, *Pins and
Needles*, before going on to roles in *The Iceman Cometh* and *Death of
a Salesman*. After having been confined to barrooms in the O'Neill
and Miller, he was pleased to get his first whiff of "fresh air on
stage." And Pat Rooney, Jr. (Arvide Abernathy), a white-haired,
snub-nosed, little man with twinkling blue eyes, who looked
like Jiggs of comic-book fame, had show biz in his genes,
being the son of a famous comedian who could (in the son's
words) "dance light as a feather in wooden shoes." The senior
Rooney had perished from pneumonia which he contracted
after rushing out of a Wilmington theatre between acts in order to get some beer. Wanting to die in New York, he boarded
a train in a black suit and breathed his last the minute the

conductor yelled "New York!" at Pennsylvania Station. Rooney, Jr. was only ten at the time, but consoled his mother: "Don't worry. I'll make more money than Dad." This is precisely what he proceeded to do after playing in vaudeville, nightclubs, and on television.

But that was the cream of the supporting crop. Stubby Kaye (Nicely Nicely), Johnny Silver (Benny Southstreet), and B.S. Pully (Big Jule) were a trio of apparent incongruities. Silver had plenty of experience in musicals (from burlesque and operetta to grand opera and pop concerts), but he had no matching experience in legitimate theatre. Stubby Kaye had been one of Major Bowes' amateur prodigies before touring across the country with impersonations of Lionel Barrymore, Fats Waller, and some far less commonly-known figures. Billed as "An Extra Padded Attraction," he had appeared in nightclubs and theatres across the country and in Canada, and these stints—along with his wartime USO tours to Greenland, Iceland, North Africa, and Sicily—had given him rigorous schooling in show biz. "It was murder, but great schooling," he commented. His *Guys and Dolls* audition was memorable because he was given more than the usual polite attention. After his prepared song, he was asked to sing another—faster, louder, and in a higher key. He thought that the casting crew were after a little mid-afternoon entertainment at his expense, especially when Frank Loesser kept moving to the rear of the theatre and then to the balcony while urging "Louder!" But after his special effort, Kaye was told: "Okay, you're Nicely-Nicely Johnson," though he wasn't sure what this meant.

The oddest man in the trio was B.S. Pully, and not simply because of his first two initials. Born Murray Lerman and raised in Newark, he had a gravel voice caused by a growth in his throat. This physical oddity had provoked his school chums to explosions of laughter whenever he recited in class. It was perhaps inevitable that he gravitated towards comedy as a performer. He started his career on amateur nights, at circuses, carnivals, and on the Borscht Belt in the Catskills, before graduating to burlesque. From there he went to Hollywood and played small roles in more than thirty films in the company of such stars as Betty Grable, James Dunne, Vivian Blaine, and George Raft. Then he turned to nightclubs and blue humour.

Pully got into *Guys and Dolls* by accident when a comedian friend, Gene Bayliss, requested his company at the audition. When Pully entered the theatre auditorium, he noticed another friend on the other side of the stage and hailed him in his gravel tones. Kaufman heard the remarkable voice, looked at him with bright eyes and asked: "Do you think you could do a role where you have to play dice?" Pully immediately pulled out a pair from his pocket and replied: "You're faded!"

Once engaged for the part, Pully remarked with utter self-assurance: "If Pinza could make the changeover to Broadway musicals, so can I."

Each performer in the colourful ensemble had a rough individuality. Long before Kaufman was involved with the show, Feuer and Martin had spent at least two years planning and working on the casting. They had both wanted unusual people, "people with bumps" or characteristics that stood out recognizably. Stubby Kaye and B.S.Pully were the most striking examples of people with bumps. But there were unusual things about the four leads as well. Of this quartet, thirty-six year old Robert Alda (Sky Masterson) had the most obvious assets for a principal, having established himself as a movie box-office success with his impersonation of George Gershwin in Warner Brothers' *Rhapsody in Blue* (1945). Alda had won the role by beating out Cary Grant, John Garfield, and a host of others. Another of Major Bowes' discoveries, he had radio, burlesque, and stock company experience. Unfortunately, Hollywood had kept him under wraps between the shooting and release of *Rhapsody*, and Alda soured on film, especially after unhappy experiences with *Cinderella Jones, April Showers,* and *The Beast With Five Fingers.* Alda fled back to New York where his Italianate glamour and easy charm served him well as Sky Masterson.

Sam Levene (Nathan Detroit) was a graduate of the American Academy of Dramatic Art, and he had a long list of notable theatre credits dating back to *Dinner at Eight, Three Men On a Horse,* and *Room Service.* He had repeated his stage role in *Three Men,* following it up with parts in *The Thin Man* and *Yellow Jack.* Hollywood directors and producers had argued that he should Anglicize his name, which had originally been Lehvinne from his Russian ancestry. With his rugged force and personality, he was quickly typecast as either a Jewish or Italian or Bronx character. Only once in his professional life had he played a romantic lead and that was long ago in 1927 in a play called *Spring Song* which flopped. In film, too, his only attempt at such a role had an unhappy fate when, after watching rushes of a movie in which Levene held Barbara Stanwyck in his arms at the fadeout, the producers yelled for a different ending.

Levene was better suited to parts of frustrated New York mugs who were always trying to scrounge up enough money for rent or grocery bills. Damon Runyon had been one of Levene's earliest fans and had promised that if the Broadway stories were sold to network radio, he would award Levene the male lead. The only problem, though a crucial one, was the fact that Levene had never before sung in a show. This worried the actor as much as it did Loesser. Nervous about his audition, Levene confessed his musical inadequacy to Abe Burrows who tried to cheer him up: "Aw, c'mon, Sam. It's going to be great and you're going to be great." The more Levene protested that he couldn't sing, the more Burrows consoled him: "Aw, come on. You don't have to be a great singer. Look at me. I can't sing, but I work nightclubs." Burrows finally managed to coax him into singing the one song that Levene thought he could pass off. This was "Pony Boy." But as the actor delivered the first line on one very flat note, Burrows was stunned into a long, thoughtful silence. "We'll work it out," he added encouragingly, even as he wondered how Frank Loesser would survive Levene's utterly unmelodious singing.

Levene's formal audition was at the St. James Theater. He insisted that nobody be present except the director, writers, and producers. When he discovered Ray Bolger in attendance, Levene refused to audition, so Bolger fled and hid in the dark balcony. After Levene had somehow croaked his way through "Pony Boy," a sad-eyed Loesser asked rhetorically: "This is 'Pony Boy,' Sam?" But everybody, including Loesser, knew that Levene was the perfect actor for Nathan Detroit, and that it was far easier to scale down the musical requirements for the role than to substitute a better singer who couldn't act the part.

The female leads brought problems of a different nature. Vivian Blaine was spotted by Feuer and Martin in June, 1950, when the producers were strolling down 54th Street in New York. Fluffy-haired and blonde at the time, she was jouncing along on shapely legs, and although she was loaded down with packages, she looked cute. "Why, it's Vivian Blaine without her red hair!" they gasped. The actress turned her blue eyes to them and said how nice it was to see them again. Feuer and Martin had disappointed her in Hollywood when she auditioned for the part of Sarah Brown. They had told her she was too strong in voice and appearance for the prim ingénue. Now she amiably put that out of her mind as she chatted politely with them before marching into her hotel, her hair and packages misbehaving. Then Martin said to her: "You know, you'd be wonderful as a honkytonk stripper." "I beg your pardon?" "I mean, how'd you like to play the comedienne, Miss Adelaide?" "I'll try anything once."

"So help me," said Feuer privately to Martin, "she looks like Adelaide."

"You're right," agreed Martin. "Let's call Loesser."

After spending several hours preparing her for the audition, Loesser was strangely silent about her progress. Two months after the Broadway opening, Blaine reminisced about the coaching, when she worked with Loesser an hour for each of three days. "He had written the words of 'Adelaide's Lament'—very clever ones, including tongue-twisters like 'psychosomatic symptoms.' But the music was only in his head, so he played it for me and I learned it by ear. He told me if the song went right, maybe they would change the part of Miss Adelaide to fit me."

The day of the tryout at the St. James, with Burrows, Feuer, Martin, Loesser, and Blaine's agent (Manny Frank) in attendance, Blaine solved the casting problem for Miss Adelaide. The moment she began "Adelaide's Lament" in her false, pinched-in tones, she made whole-hearted enthusiasts of her audience. Abe Burrows commented: "She fractured us. You're usually cagey at these auditions because if the gal is good, it'll cost you money if you get too excited—so you just say, 'How nice!' even if you adore her, and you never, never applaud." But this time, Burrows, Feuer, and Martin couldn't restrain themselves. They applauded and said, "You're terrific!"

Frank Loesser finally broke his silence about Blaine: "I knew it the first time I heard her. I wanted to surprise you."

Manny Frank quickly negotiated terms of a contract, but Blaine left for some summer theatre engagements without actually signing for Guys and Dolls. Casting had to be approved by George Kaufman who was still in France at the time, and when informed about developments over a bad transatlantic telephone connection, he remarked, "She's not right for the part," and urged them to find someone else. Discouraged, Feuer and Martin suspended negotiations and ignored Manny Frank's frantic phone calls, but as soon as Kaufman's ship docked in New York, the producers rushed aboard to argue their case. As it transpired, Kaufman had confused Blaine with another actress, and a contract was duly mailed to Vivian Blaine.

The irony was that when Blaine read the finished script later, she was disappointed: "Adelaide didn't seem like much of a part—only a spot here, a spot there, and two or three songs. I said,'Only those few scenes?' But my husband said, 'Wait and see.'"

Born Vivian Stapleton in 1923 in Newark, New Jersey, she was the daughter of a jovial, husky Irishman, a bookkeeper and auto-supply salesman whose first love was show biz. Lionel Stapleton spent most of his time booking talent for local clubs and taking an occasional turn himself as a song-and-dance man. Sensing his daughter's talent, he introduced her at three to an American Legion audience, for whom she danced the charleston and black bottom and sang "Roll On, Mississippi, Roll On." Even when her parents divorced, her father booked singing dates for her at $1 a night. Still in elementary school, she sang at fraternal affairs, nightclubs, company benefits, and police benefits. She was first introduced to the microphone at Club Evergreen in Bloomfield, New Jersey, where, in black velvet shorts, white satin blouse, and a black velvet tam, she blasted her audience out of their seats with a deafening version of "Red Sails in the Sunset." The volume and register were encouraged by her father who always advised singers: "It might not be good, but it's got to be loud!"

At fourteen, Vivian became a vocalist for Halsey Miller's orchestra, singing three or four nights a week for $5 a night. After graduating from Southside High School in Newark, she went on the road with various, little-known bands, singing rhythm numbers, ballads, marches, and even hymns. She received her first big break after a newspaper publicity photo was spotted by Meyer Mishkin, a talent scout for Twentieth Century-Fox. "Get in touch with me after you lose some weight," Mishkin advised, and he continued to call her while secretly plotting with her mother to make Vivian reduce. When she did make her screen test in December, 1941, and was offered $100 a week by Darryl F. Zanuck, she finally realized the need to diet. As Arthur D. Morse reported, she noticed scores of slim starlets who "looked as though they had all been poured from the same mold." Spurred to a regimen of exercise and dieting, she became frustrated when her surplus pounds refused to disappear. At one point, she was given such violent massages that when Zanuck asked to see her in a bathing suit, she wore dark stockings to camouflage the black-and-blue marks.

The result was a set of inconspicuous roles in three inconspicuous films, and then a six-month hiatus without another picture. During the layoff, she played the USO camp-show circuit six nights a week, winning the attention of Manny Frank who was already a well-known agent. He rushed to represent her, winning her spots on bills with Frank Sinatra and Betty Hutton, though he could do little to make Twentieth Century-Fox advance her movie career. Vivian, however, took matters into her own hand when she stormed into Zanuck's office and demanded her immediate release unless he was prepared to offer her work. The startled tycoon ordered her tested, along with thirty-nine other girls, for the lead in a Technicolor musical, Greenwich Village. She won the role and was promptly dubbed "The Cherry Blonde," going on to impress Walter Winchell and others who nicknamed her "Miss Pin-Up Perfection" and "Lo-Lo-Lita, Sweetheart of the Army."

Marriage to Manny Frank followed and record-breaking nightclub appearances across the country. She appeared to be in a position to rival June Haver and Betty Grable. But Vivian was determined to stay away from Hollywood unless she was offered better roles. In the summer of 1948, she electrified audiences in Dallas when she played the lead in One Touch of Venus, revealing a sly humour that would eventually become her trademark, though never more colourfully than it would in Guys and Dolls.

When rehearsals began, Burrows expanded her part. Herbert Greene, the vocal director and arranger, remembers her being the only singer he didn't have to work with. "She was so good that there just wasns't anything I could say to her." Choreographer Michael Kidd was amazed at her dexterity in learning his dances. "At first I thought she might dance half a chorus and stay in the background, but she shook her head and learned the whole works. She was so determined to be perfect that I had to force her to rest. I never saw anyone who worked so hard."

Blaine took her role so seriously that during the Broadway run, she began to show the physical symptoms of Miss Adelaide: a psychosomatic cold and post-nasal drip. "I had a cold the first six months of the show, but it was all in my mind. I went to the doctors and they made with their pipes and sprays and told me I simply did NOT have a cold. I really got kind of schizophrenic about it."

Sarah Brown was an entirely different problem. The role was difficult to cast because it required a young, beautiful ingénue with a soprano voice who could handle Loesser's sprinkling of high notes. Hundreds of aspiring singers and actresses had failed to satisfy the director and librettist. However, while Kaufman and Burrows were pouring over the script at Kaufman's Bucks County home just a week before rehearsals, they received a phone-call from Ernie Martin who believed he had found the right girl. Loesser had auditioned her and approved of her singing, and Martin was anxious to sign her quickly. If Kaufman agreed, Martin would drive her down to Bucks County that evening and have her read the part.

Unfortunately, Martin had no map and got lost, arriving with his "discovery" around midnight when Kaufman and Burrows and their respective wives were weary from the long wait. Equally weary and far more worried were Martin and Isabel Bigley. Despite being frightened half to death, however, the young actress made an attractive impression on Carin Burrows and Leueen (MacGrath) Kaufman who both nodded their approval to their mates. A tired Kaufman was kind to Bigley, though he hurried the audition, giving her only a single scene to read, a romantic one at that, which she did as Burrows played Sky Masterson. The incongruous pairing did not throw her off any more than did the country house setting or the late hour. Kaufman,however, had no more stamina. Raising his hand wearily, he mumbled, "That's fine, that's fine," as if intent on terminating proceedings summarily so that he could stumble into bed. Martin bade a quick goodnight to all, packed Bigley into his car, and returned to New York.

Isabel Bigley proved to be perfect as the Mission doll. A brown-haired beauty, with grey-blue eyes and a wide forehead, she was only twenty-two at the time and had limited, though significant, professional experience. She learned music from her mother, a contralto who had won many medals for her singing in her home country, Northern Ireland. Bigley's father loved music too. He had a tenor voice, and he and his wife sang in the choir of an Episcopalian church in New York. Young Isabel had been a member of the junior choir before being promoted to soprano soloist. Soon she was having lessons from Mrs. William Neidlinger while also majoring in musical theory and practice at Walton High School. She was the only pupil accepted from her school by the All City Chorus, whose director, Peter J. Wilhousky, urged her to study at the Juilliard School during her vacations. She followed his urging, also learning stenography and typing, which her father said would support her while she was trying to break into theatre. Her stenography landed her a job with the insurance firm of Lukens, Savage and Washburn, which generously granted her time off so that she could sing for people as long as she could make up this time later. That's how she got to audition as chorus singer and understudy for Laurey in *Okla-*

homa! Her audition with Richard Rodgers took longer than expected, so she telephoned her office to say that it was too late for her to return to work that day. As it transpired, she never returned, plunging instead into *Oklahoma!* She made such a strong impression in a few weeks that the producers dispatched her to London where she stayed for three years.

Howard Hughes asked her to do a screen test, but before she could comply, she met Cy Feuer who had seen her picture in *Time.* Feuer invited her to lunch in Beverly Hills and said, "You look like a mission lass, and I mean that to be a compliment." He asked her to audition for *Guys and Dolls*, but because she hadn't sung in two months and was afraid to perform in the cavernous Los Angeles Philharmonic Auditorium, she turned him down. Her screen test for Hughes turned into a fiasco. The studio big-wigs somehow pictured her as a sultry blues singer, a sort of Ava Gardner, which she most certainly wasn't. Hughes liked her, but his advisers claimed that she couldn't sing very well, didn't act very well, and photographed like "something less than a million dollars." The next day, a bizarre accident changed her fortunes. While crossing a busy Hollywood intersection, she was struck by a car whose jutting hood ornament pierced her elbow. While recuperating, she was asked by Hughes to stick around Hollywood because something might pop up. But she lied, "I can't wait around here, because I'm committed to *Guys and Dolls*." So, instead of collecting $350 a week from Hughes for doing nothing, she headed back to New York to arrange for a return to a London nightclub date, and that's when her agent contacted her with the news that Feuer and Martin wanted her to sing for Frank Loesser.

It was six in the evening when she arrived at the theatre for her audition and heard another girl singing. The rival was good, and Bigley knew she had serious competition. When her turn came, she did a love song, after which Feuer, Martin, and Loesser asked if she could do something hot. So she took the only other song she'd brought along and tried changing it as an experiment in the sultry. Sarah Brown had two sorts of songs, and the producers were looking for someone who could sing both tenderly and sensually. She was the right girl for the role, and they arranged for her to be released from her other commitments.

Rehearsals weren't easy for her, however. Hired three days before rehearsal, she was certain the production would be a hit, but she wondered if she would be good enough. Claudia Franck, her drama coach, put her misgivings to rest: "Who are you to think you can learn everything in the theater in three years?" The young actress settled down and responded well to Kaufman's direction.

Kaufman was rather professorial. As Burrows relates, "He looked scholarly and he dressed casually. When he was directing the actors he was a businesslike professor in his speech and manner. He showed it on the first day of rehearsal." As the cast members were introduced to one another and sat at a long table with scripts in front of them, Kaufman simply opened his script and said, "Act One, Scene One." No analysis of the play or characters, no preliminary remarks about the technical aspects of the production. The cast went through the entire play without being interrupted even once by Kaufman.

The director maintained a fairly cool distance between himself and the cast, practising a civility that earned him great respect. It was always Mister Levene, Miss Blaine, Mister Alda, Miss Bigley, Mister Pully. Never first names. Even friends and colleagues were addressed as Mister Burrows, Mister Loesser, et cetera. And, of course, he was always addressed as Mister Kaufman.

Sam Levene was annoyed by the formality. Instead of calling his director "Mister Kaufman," he addressed him as "Sir" in a tone of mock humility. When he wished to ask a question about a scene, he would approach the edge of the stage and call out a loud "Sir?" as Kaufman answered quietly, "Yes, Mister Levene?" This invariably disarmed Levene of his mockery and irritation.

Kaufman was just as firm with an audience. As Burrows wandered around the theatre, checking sightlines, particularly for crowd scenes, and complained, "Mister Kaufman, in those seats on the left, the people sitting there won't be able to see her while she's singing," Kaufman's response was "Well, they shouldn't be sitting there."

Eventually, Burrows learned what Kaufman meant. "In order to make a scene look right and have *everyone* in the whole theater see *everyone* on the stage, the actors would have to stand in a long, uninteresting, straight line." Kaufman deliberately broke this stilted blocking, even if it meant that an audience would have to see backs of actors for brief periods.

Kaufman worked calmly and easily. Tantrums and wild rantings were never parts of his style. When he needed to reprove an actor, he did so with exquisite control—as in the case of Tom Pedi, who in an attempt to enlarge laughs as Harry the Horse was taking immense liberties with the script. Burrows was annoyed but kept his silence. One day, as Burrows recounts, Pedi invented "a whole new sentence on the way to a joke." The librettist fumed in the back row as Pedi's invention ruined a good laugh line. Kaufman stopped the rehearsal, walked over to the actor, put a hand on his shoulder, and called out in the dark theatre, "Is Mr. Burrows out there?" "I'm back here, Mr. Kaufman," came the reply. "Mr. Burrows, I've been listening to Mr. Pedi. Would you consider giving him credit as co-author?" Burrows answered pleasantly, "I'll think about it," and the whole company laughed. Pedi never ad-libbed again.

However, Kaufman knew and respected an actor's importance to interpretation, and in another instance he allowed Tom Pedi to deliver a line in a way that was wildly different from that intended by Burrows. A startled Burrows jumped out of his seat, but was restrained by Kaufman who remarked, "Let him alone. His reading is better than yours." (When Pedi delivered that line before an audience, he received tremendous laughter and Burrows got credit for a great line.)

The actors were sometimes excessively in awe of their director. During rehearsals for the Philadelphia tryout, Vivian Blaine went to Burrows with a problem. Bothered by a line of dialogue, she asked him how he thought she should handle the speech and the little bit of business connected with it. "Why don't you ask Mr. Kaufman?" Burrows replied. Blaine looked at him with horror and remarked, "I wouldn't ask him." As a newcomer to Broadway musicals, she felt insecure and daunted. When she did muster courage to approach Kaufman, she was soothed and never feared him again, although, like her acting colleagues, she never regarded him as a buddy.

Kaufman was patient with everything, except tardiness. Punctuality had always been a distinguishing trait of his conduct, and he expected no less from cast and crew. He himself never arrived late, though he never stayed a minute past 4 p.m. Burrows claims that Kaufman simply vanished, without a "Goodbye" or "So long" or "See you later," and so unobtrusively that nobody figured out how he did it. Kaufman kept everyone so busy that nobody had time to consult a watch—nobody but Kaufman himself, who would take note of the time, then drift to the rear of the theatre at exactly five minutes to four, and disappear while the crew and actors were immersed in their rehearsal.

It was widely suspected that Kaufman joined his bridge club every afternoon at four.

Punctuality was allied to professionalism. As Abe Burrows claims, Kaufman felt very strongly that "before actors came to work with him, they should be professionals." Kaufman once remarked, "Abe, I don't run an acting school." The director wanted to use rehearsal time for concentrating on the flow of dramatic action, on guiding the actors to an understanding of their roles, not on teaching them the basics of acting. It was disconcerting to Kaufman to have performers who seemed more interested in singing than in acting, for he was never terribly interested in the music.

Musical problems, however, had to be resolved and sometimes in concert with egos. Sam Levene, for example, was upset at being told not to sing during group numbers because of his lack of tone. The musical arrangements were difficult, and Levene couldn't harmonize with the others. One day during a rehearsal break, he announced that he wasn't entirely tone-deaf. He claimed that he simply needed help to sing in tune, and he offered to demonstrate. Requesting that Feuer, Loesser, and Burrows sit out front, he asked the rehearsal pianist to hit a note that he would match vocally. The pianist sounded an A. Levene sang his idea of A which, as Burrows describes, was "wildly off-key." Levene looked out hopefully, but Feuer, Loesser, and Burrows all shook their heads. This went on six times, with Levene doggedly singing wrong A's. Eventually, on the eighth attempt, a miracle occurred, a true A issued from his mouth. Feuer, Loesser, and Burrows applauded. As they congratulated him, "You got it, Sam," the actor beamed. But then Levene said, "Do it again." It was a fatal self-confidence. Levene tried and tried, missing the note every time. Not only was he singing the wrong note; sometimes he would produce no discernible note at all. Suddenly, he walked down to the foot of the stage and shouted, "I know what you three are doing! It's a lousy trick! You guys have agreed every single time. It ain't possible that you always agree on what's the right note. It was a trick."

But Levene had to admit defeat in another song as well. "Travelling Light" had been composed for Nathan and Sky in both 3/4 and 5/4 time so that the free and easy male leads could be established. But Levene couldn't learn the song.

Neither key nor rhythm came to his ear or lips, and the actor eventually grew so exasperated in rehearsals that he would stomp his foot midway into the first chorus and shout, "Stop! I don't know where I am!" He and everyone else on stage would cringe until the number was over. Feuer and Kaufman both knew that Levene would never get the song right, but because they loved the number they allowed him to slog his way painfully through it.

When New York previews began, Burrows worked patiently in a corner with Levene, but even he was forced to admit to Kaufman "Take it out. He'll never be able to do it."

The next day, Feuer assembled the entire cast on stage and announced, "As of tonight's performance, we're cutting 'Travelling Light.' It's out. Everybody re-adjust to it. 'Travelling Light' is OUT." And without giving Levene a chance to object ("Waddya cutting it for?"), Feuer ran out of the theatre and jumped into a waiting cab.

Levene was forced to accept "with middling good grace" (in Burrows' phrase) the loss of all his songs, with the exception of "Sue Me." And that number, too, was almost ruined by Levene's habit of coming in on the wrong note. Loesser added "call a lawyer" and in an ascending five-note phrase to give the actor the means (in Susan Loesser's words) "to slide up to a relatively accurate starting point." The number finally worked, purely on the strength of Levene's acting and the strong orchestral accompaniment which did its best to disguise Levene's flat notes.

Kaufman knew that Levene could more than compensate for musical deficiency by his colourful characterization, although he commanded that the actor merely mouth the words to "The Oldest Established."

Levene was not the only one in the cast who was beset by problems. During the Philadelphia rehearsals, Isabel Bigley found herself the target of Frank Loesser's violent wrath. She had been trying to make "If I Were a Bell" sound the way Loesser had wanted it, but she failed to satisfy the composer who finally jumped up on a riser that put him at her eye-level, and slapped her in the face.

Everyone froze in horrible shock. The stricken actress went home. Loesser was immediately contrite and attempted to mend things by a gift of flowers and jewellery. But when the actress did return to rehearsals, she kept her distance from Loesser. The song still failed to work, and Kaufman and Loesser tried various means of solving the problem, including one that had Vivian Blaine do it "down-in-one" during a set change while she was lounging on a couch with a telephone to her mouth. This resource was misjudged, if nothing else, for what was a frustrated chorus-girl doing singing a number that was appropriate only to a young lady with "a quiet upbringing" who was suddenly in love with a notorious gambler?

"What the hell is Miss Adelaide doing singing 'Bell' in that silly position?" Loesser's wife asked. "Who in the name of God is she talking to—and why is she singing that song at all?"

When Loesser countered that Bigley couldn't sing it, his wife insisted otherwise: "I say she can. You can teach her." To which the composer sheepishly retorted: "She won't talk to me since I hit her."

Somehow his wife convinced him to attempt a reconciliation with the actress, and the next morning Loesser was seen standing on two phone books, nose to nose with his Sarah Brown, coaching her through the song.

Loesser's notorious temper was displayed yet again during a rehearsal of "The Oldest Established," though this episode was shot through with idiosyncratic humour. As Cy Feuer recalled, the composer had the male singers rehearsing the number for two days with the conductor. The Erlanger Theater had a long orchestra and a long lobby that ran all the way to the street. Michael Kidd, the choreographer, wishing to be considerate, advised his cast to save their voices while he blocked the number. The actors willingly complied, only to hear Loesser yelling as he charged down the aisle, "What the hell is going on here? Goddammit, we rehearsed all day yesterday, and now what do I hear? Nothing! This is the worst goddamn thing!" Contemptuously dismissive of both Feuer and Kidd, he roared, "I want to hear the goddamned song the way I rehearsed it—and I want to hear it NOW!"

As the male chorus promptly started to follow his decree, Loesser backed up the aisle all the way to the rear of the auditorium and just stood there, listening. Then he turned around and headed for the lobby, as Feuer ran up one aisle and Kidd the other to open the doors for him. With the chorus still singing their hearts out, Loesser walked out into the street, turned right, and went nextdoor to an ice-cream store. Feuer concludes the story: "We're watching him from the theater entrance as he buys an ice cream cone and walks on down the street to his hotel. Meanwhile, the guys are still singing."

By contrast, Kaufman remained equanimous. Nothing seemed to deter him in the final analysis—neither an actor's insecurity about a dance routine, nor another's overly-creative experiment with makeup. Pat Rooney was eager to perform a well-remembered waltz clog form his vaudeville days, but the pretty number was all wrong for this show. The sight of a gentle, grey-haired missionary suddenly breaking into a waltz clog was jarring. Knowing that Rooney would be hurt by the decision to cut one of his signature routines, Kaufman had to be tactful yet firm. He found a way by having Loesser write another song for Rooney, the lovely, tender "More I Cannot Wish You," sung to his granddaughter, Sarah Brown.

The makeup incident revealed Kaufman's talent for well-judged crisis-handling. B.S. Pully, the huge, gravel-voiced actor with the formidable presence, knew all his lines and never missed a cue. But he indulged himself with makeup by increasing the amount of eye shadow, lipstick, and rouge so that he looked alarmingly like one about to go out for Trick or Treat on Halloween. Everyone complained to Kaufman who kept promising, "I'll take care of it." But there were no outward signs of intercession until the New York opening when the director called a very brief rehearsal in the morning and then ended it with a matchingly brief remark: "I know you'll all be fine tonight, and if I don't come backstage to see you, it's because I don't like crowds." As the actors began to leave the stage, he stopped Pully and said quietly, "Mr. Pully, you're doing very well, but if I were you, I would leave off all that makeup." That quiet advice was all that was needed. On opening night, Big Jule entered perfectly in character, without any hint of wild makeup, and went on to become (in Burrows' words) "one of the funniest villains of all time."

Kaufman later told Burrows that he knew Pully's makeup was bothering everybody, but he added, "If I'd've told him to leave it off last week, he would have had it all back by tonight."

As usual, Kaufman's tone and timing were impeccable.

# PHILADELPHIA

**ABE BURROWS** declared that four days before the cast and crew left for a Philadelphia tryout in early October, "something magical seemed to happen to the show." He himself was affected by the magic for he found himself actually enjoying the rehearsals. "All the scattered pieces began to become one beautiful unit." What had been a "loosely fragmented project"—as is usually the case with a musical—became "a real show." Michael Kidd's dance scenes and the book scenes blended together seamlessly; and the actors had such ease and authority that they moved as if they actually owned the stage. George Kaufman's brilliance was especially evident in "The Crap Game Dance," where Kidd choreographed a real crap game with twenty gamblers, "some of them rolling the dice, others engaged in arguments," and the entire action structured by Kaufman with the finesse of "a master jeweler assembling a watch."

However, Burrows was soon to learn that his "wildly enthusiastic reaction" to those rehearsals before the Philadelphia tryout was "a common theatrical disease called Pre-Philadelphia Hallucination, a virulent form of self-delusion."

Originally selected because of its cosmopolitan audience, Philadelphia was, as Burrows pointed out, far enough from New York so that it discouraged the Broadway crowd from coming down to enjoy the production's problems.

Burrows felt uneasy though he and Kaufman were quickly treated like celebrities when they walked down Broad Street for they were recognized from their appearances on the television show, *This Is Show Business*. Kaufman disliked vulgar public adulation. "What are we supposed to be, goldfish in a bowl?" he complained acidly. Burrows smirked: "George, you were the one who chose to go on TV. These are your fans. They adore you. Why don't you just relax and enjoy it?" Kaufman grunted contemptuously.

His contempt turned to utter shock later in a restaurant when (with Burrows as a witness) a lady approached his table, declaring, "I can't help myself" as she suddenly ruffled his hair with both her hands. Then she fled as Kaufman sat, his hair standing on edge, "as though someone had just electrocuted him."

The initial rehearsals at the Shubert Theater were bedlam because the actors had their first exposure to the real sets. Lines were blown, lyrics forgotten as the cast, busily tried to open doors that stuck or move around without stumbling into furniture or bumping into stagehands. Everyone was ill at ease in the new space. Burrows was painfully embarrassed as his dialogue and jokes sounded dreadful. However, the next rehearsal marked a recovery as the cast had an orchestra in the pit for the very first time. The musicians made all the difference in the world for singers and actors, because not only did they provide cues, they also responded spontaneously to the jokes. As Burrows explained in his memoir: "Laughter is the electricity that makes a comedy writer's blood start pumping. The musicians are the only people in the theater who have never heard the jokes before, and they laugh and it makes us— and the actors—feel a lot better."

It was during the Philadelphia rehearsals that the famous slap and ice-cream incidents with Loesser occurred, and which have already been recounted. The first dress rehearsal brought the usual complaints from cast members. "My shoes are too tight." "Am I going to have to wear this thing?" "Are you trying to make me look ugly?" One of the Hat Box girls, embarrassed by her scanty costume, walked to the front of the stage and said," I can't go on the stage like this. I look almost naked." But one of the producers yelled back from the auditorium, "That's the whole idea."

Burrows remembers the rehearsal turning into "a sort of hostile fashion show," with the producers solemnly promising to fix all the shoes and costumes to everyone's satisfaction. With all the grunts and groans quelled, and with everyone pretending to be pleased, these crises passed. But what was supposed to have been the final dress rehearsal was so disastrous that there had to be yet another "dress." With the story refusing to take life in the first act, the pace dragged. This turned the cast so glum that despite the improvement of the second act, their mood remained despondent. The producers, composer, and musicians decided that the book needed deep cutting in the very opening scene. Burrows resisted this notion at first, and received some comfort from Kaufman who, having suffered patiently through many bad rehearsals in his career, refused to panic. The director felt that no major changes should be made until an audience had seen the show. A vehement argument ensued, involving Feuer, Martin, Kidd, Burrows, and Kaufman, as they all stood at the rear of the theater, with their voices growing in volume. So vociferous was the sharp exchange of views that the actors, who had been instructed to wait for notes on their performances, felt their own nerves on edge. Their misery was only partially allayed when the stage manager finally dismissed them with the injunction to return an hour early for an evening rehearsal.

Meanwhile, as the argument raged within the auditorium, Burrows felt excessively hammered about his libretto. He looked helplessly at Kaufman, but knew that the famous "show doctor" couldn't be his own "doctor" and remedy a situation in which he was so firmly involved. Burrows finally blurted out, "George, maybe we can go back to the hotel and find a few cuts in the opening stuff." Surveying his partners with some disdain, Kaufman shrugged and remarked: "You're all a bunch of amateurs." Then he walked out, with Burrows following in close pursuit.

Back at Kaufman's hotel room, as Burrows recalls, the two "performed some radical surgery on the opening section of the show," though Burrows was embarrassed about having to make radical cuts in the key exposition. "I remembered when George had lectured me on this subject and told me I should take my time, lay the story out clearly, and the audience would hold still for it." But he did make the cuts and give them to the actors who stifled their own displeasure at having to make adjustments so late into production.

The second "final" rehearsal took place before a small invited audience of friends, agents, and wives. It turned into a fiasco that made the previous rehearsal seem (in Burrows' words) "like a dazzling hit." Apart from Michael Kidd's opening ballet—always a hit at every performance—nothing else seemed to work. Burrows was disturbed: "We had taken out the so-called dull spots in the opening scene and the rest of the show just rolled over and died. There was practically no laughs, no excitement. Just nothing."

By the final curtain, Burrows and his colleagues all knew that they had committed "theatrical malpractice." The producers, Kaufman, and Burrows held a panic-stricken meeting after enjoining the weary actors to hold back in the theatre for further changes that very night. Kaufman was incensed about recommendations to restore what had been cut. After fuming aloud, he abruptly turned on his heel and left. The poor actors, however, had no recourse but to accept the new alterations at one in the morning and then practically stagger to their hotel rooms.

Sam Levene was the only one who still had reserves of energy for protest. He was infuriated at having to be subject to the producers' vacillations. First he had lost some of his favourite lines; now he had to relearn those and forget the rewrites. Pointing his finger at Burrows, he exclaimed dramatically: "Abe, it's very important for this show that I should be happy. And I'm miserable!" As the actor stalked out in quasi-Shakespearean choler, Burrows stood there for an instant before suddenly bursting into what he called "moderate hysteria."

The next day, Kaufman called a brief run-through for the afternoon. The company was generally grumpy, with Sam Levene still visibly unhappy about developments. But now the usually cheerful Robert Alda had become discontented as well. He complained to Burrows: "Everyone else in the show is getting laughs and I'm a straight man." "You were great as George Gershwin in *Rhapsody In Blue*, and you didn't get laughs in that," Burrows responded, adding that Alda was the leading man, the handsome hero whom all the women (including Burrows' wife) thought was beautiful. Burrows assured him that many lines which didn't seem to be laugh lines at rehearsal would receive big laughs from a real audience. Alda muttered that he would play the role of Sky as written but that he hoped Burrows would write him "some funny stuff" after the Philadelphia opening.

Burrows was on the receiving end of other complaints— one of which was touching. A male singer pleaded, "Mr. Burrows, could I please have a name?" Initially puzzled by this request, Burrows realized that the singer, merely listed as "a horseplayer" for the "Fugue for Tin Horns," didn't have any dialogue in the book and didn't have a character name. The actor was particularly aggrieved that his fellow-singers had distinctive monikers: Nicely-Nicely Johnson and Bennie Southstreet. Perusing his Runyon once again, Burrows discovered the name of Rusty Charlie, and passed it on to the relieved actor.

Opening night in Philadelphia filled Burrows with particular dread when the local critics were pointed out to him as they arrived at the Shubert. He was hardly soothed by nervous friends who had loyally come down from New York in order to be his claque. When the houselights dimmed, he felt "like the bull in a bullfight at the Moment of Truth." He glanced at George Kaufman, Feuer, and Martin, and Frank Loesser, and they all seemed to be more composed that he was. All the excitement he had first experienced working on the show dissolved into terror. His wife, Carin, who held his hands in the very last row, thought his face had actually turned *green*.

Then the overture started and was applauded. The curtain rose on Jo Mielziner's Times Square scene, and the audience clapped appreciatively again. Michael Kidd's opening street scene ballet went without a hitch and it, too, got nice applause. All the omens seemed fine, but Burrows was still anxious. He didn't have to worry long, for as the three horseplayers, Nicely-Nicely, Benny Southstreet, and Rusty Charlie, strolled to center stage with their racing forms, a solo trumpet in the orchestra played the First Call heard before a big race. The audience shook with the laughter of "instant recognition," and Burrows realized that they weren't simply laughing at a joke-line but at the characters, milieu, and situation. At the final curtain, the audience went mad, shouting and screaming its approval. Turning to his wife, Burrows kissed her on the cheek and said: "We're home."

Then he left his seat to stand at the rear of the orchestra stalls and found he was not alone. George Kaufman was there, pacing up and down, as were Feuer, Martin, and Loesser. Burrows joined them and recalled later: "I was pacing on air. I sure was high. The audience seemed to be laughing at every line and cheering every number."

The intermission brought hearty applause. Kaufman and Burrows were mobbed by friends and television fans, which led Kaufman to flee in his usual disapproving way. When Burrows went backstage to greet the actors, Robert Alda hurried over to him and said exuberantly, "Hey, Abe, did you hear those big boffos I got?" Burrows replied smugly: "I told you, didn't I?"

When Burrows and his wife took their seats for the second act, they wondered whether the show could sustain its quality, especially as the second-half was much longer than was customary for a musical. But soon after the curtain went up, the audience was relishing the production, and a relieved Burrows kissed his wife on the cheek as he got up to resume his pacing at the rear of the theatre. Burrows recalled: "As I paced, I started congratulating myself. I was full of self-admiration. I kept thinking, 'Why haven't I been doing this sort of thing all my life? This Broadway stuff is a cinch.'"

His buoyant euphoria continued the next morning after the rave reviews, congratulatory phone calls, and telegrams. Max Gordon wired: "Dear Abe. Bend down and pick up the money."

Only Isabel Bigley failed to catch the celebratory mood after the final curtain. Taking her bows, she flashed smiles, but as the curtain rang down for the night, she burst into tears and rushed off the stage. Fellow actors gathered around her in her dressing room, before the wardrobe mistress bustled them all out and explained to the producers that she had discovered the source of Miss Bigley's unhappiness. She fished out a letter from her apron pocket. It was from a former schoolfriend: "Dear Isabel, It is so wonderful to hear the news of your big chance on Broadway. I am terribly happy for you and everyone says the show will be a great hit. Remember how you always dreamed about being a star even back in high school? It's really a dream come true, and I can hardly wait to see you in all that glitter and music, and especially in all your beautiful costumes."

Fearing her friend's crushing disappointment at the plain costuming for Sarah Brown, Bigley was quite inconsolable. When her colleagues rushed to Kaufman for help, he remarked that the mood of the show was not like that of Christmas Eve at Bergdorf Goodman, but he promised to think of a plan to dry her tears.

Before the curtain on the Broadway opening night, he deposited a package on her dressing table. It contained a new shirt-waist and a ruffled collar!

"Gay and Gorgeous" ran the headline in the *Philadelphia Inquirer* of October 22, as its critic declared: "Figuratively, factually, financially, or any way you wish, 'Guys and Dolls' is a whale of a hit." Similar raves came from *The Evening Bulletin* and the *Philadelphia Daily News.Variety* gushed over the libretto: "Here's really one for the records—a musical in which the book is apparently the standout feature." Isabel Bigley, rather than the other leads, was given top marks for her singing, with *Variety*'s commenting that "the singers tend to be overshadowed by the orchestra, but that is among the faults in process of correction."

Then came a sour reminder of reality with the second night. It is only too common for a show to sag on the second night after a highly successful opening, for when the cast does not think that the second audience is as appreciative as the first, they have a tendency to push too hard, thereby forcing the pace, straining the comic effects, and perhaps even coarsening the songs. Their misconceived efforts usually deepen the disappointment, and eventually the actors panic. This is exactly what happened in *Guys and Dolls*. Robert Alda lost the big laughs he had received on opening night. At intermission he was like a balloon with all its air seeping out. He moaned: "Abe, what the hell happened? Every one of my jokes died."

Burrows and colleagues were forced to see the show in a new, cold light, one that exposed all the "holes" in what was prematurely assumed to be a hit. But Feuer and Martin wanted the show to arrive on Broadway in what they called "perfect" shape, so everyone continued to tinker with the production, which was kept in Philadelphia for six weeks, divided between two theatres, first the Shubert, and then the Erlanger, and grossing over $200,000. In *George S. Kaufman And His Friends*, Scott Meredith reports that Kaufman, fearing that his producers were beginning to lose perspective in their insistent revisions, warned them not to pander to the lowest common denominator. Martin replied that he wanted a show that would appeal not just to Broadway audiences, but to theatre-goers everywhere. "Don't degrade it," Kaufman remarked, "by throwing in more girls and stuff. I think we've got something exceptional, almost literary, in a way."

*Guys and Dolls* had one undeniable blessing in the Philadelphia tryout. It drew huge audiences, so there were no financial problems to interfere with revisions. And alterations were what went on day and night. One evening during the third week of the run, the hilarious crap game in the second act failed. It was astonishing, for this was one scene that had always worked prior to this occasion. Now, as Burrows puts it, "it just lay there like a big beached whale." But there was no available alternative, so Burrows didn't tinker with the scene. This was just as well, for whatever the reason for the sudden misery, it disappeared as mysteriously as it had appeared.

Loesser was having his own problems. The song "Travelin' Light," written for Alda and Levene, had to be cut. Loesser had been expecting a Sky who could dance, and a Nathan who could sing, but as Alda could sing but not dance, and Levene could really do neither, there was no option but to sacrifice the song.

Feuer and Martin were getting increasingly apprehensive as changes ran into the final week in Philadelphia. Kaufman suggested extending the tryout period, but this would mean postponing the New York opening. Feuer and Martin were deadset against this, but left Kaufman and Burrows to their own devices. Burrows suddenly had the idea of letting Nicely-Nicely Johnson and Benny Southstreet take over the troublesome title song. The point was to have it sung as a comment on Sky Masterson's attitude towards Sarah Brown. Kaufman was so approving of the alteration that he immediately phoned the producers, who, upon hearing of the change, decided to take another week in Philadelphia and move the show to the Erlanger.

The final touch on the show came from Loesser who had to come up with a new song to open the second act. He dug up "Take Back Your Mink," a tune he used to sing at parties, though he struggled to find a rhyming pattern. When Jule Styne came to town to see the show, he called Loesser from the hotel lobby and was told, "If you don't have any rhymes for 'mink,' don't come up."

The number was deliriously funny satire, with Adelaide and cohorts dressed to the nines in golden gowns, shoes, hats, pearl necklaces, and mink stoles. Wielding long cigarette-holders as  mark of sophistication, they were to take umbrage at the suggestion that they were to trade sex for the finery. The lyric went: "Take back your mink/Take back your pearls/What made you think/That I was one of those girls?" The new singing and dancing by the Hot Box girls meant that Kidd had to work up new choreography, and Alvin Colt to whip up more costumes. The orchestration also had to be rehearsed—all in a single week before New York.

Kaufman's big problem with the number was a purely practical matter of clearing the stage correctly once the chorines had divested themselves of hats, cigarette holders, minks, and jewels. The floor was a welter of "jools" and clothing after their exit, so how were they ever going to get the stuff sorted out? Then his genius came to the fore with a single, shrewd touch. Kaufman had the Hot Box girls come back, pick up their precious belongings which they had only just renounced in umbrage at the suggestion that they were commercial barter, look at the house, and in fine, cooing fashion ask: "Well, wooden yeousse?"

"Take Back Your Mink" was a knockout on the very last night in Philadelphia, leading to high hopes for the Broadway opening.

*Guys and Dolls*: The Happy Ending

# BROADWAY
# MUSICAL CHAMP

**WITH A TOP TICKET PRICE** of $9.60 for orchestra seats, *Guys and Dolls* opened at the 46th Street Theatre, New York, on Friday, November 24, 1950. After the warm but tentative response in Philadelphia, everyone was nervous. How would the last-minute revisions play to Broadway?

Abe Burrows stood in the rear of the theatre to meet friends and watch the critics arrive: Richard Watts, John Chapman, Howard Barnes, Wolcott Gibbs, Brooks Atkinson, George Jean Nathan, and others. As the houselights dimmed, Frank Loesser began to pace up and down the back of the house, while Carin and Abe Burrows sat in the orchestra, holding hands.

The overture was fine. The curtain rose for the opening ballet. It went smoothly enough, its eye-catching details and choreography being especially appealing to Runyon fans, those in the know about Times Square, Lindy's, bookies, and dames. Then came the bugle call, and "A Fugue for Tinhorns," and the show took off, never to look back or waver. "It was like electricity," recalled Carin Burrows. "That's when we knew we had an enormous hit. You have to experience the opening night of a really major hit to know what it feels like. There's an electricity in the audience that is palpable. You know it right away."

At intermission, the audience seemed exultant. Even the normally inscrutable critics seemed content. Richard Watts, then critic for the *New York Post*, went up to Burrows, put his arm around his shoulder and whispered: "Abe, I'm having a wonderful time...and so is Mr. Atkinson."

That would normally have been the seal of approval, but Burrows worried if the second act would make Watts and Atkinson change their minds.

He worried even through the final ovations, and on the way to the opening-night party at "21." He needn't have bothered. Friendly rooters deluged him with congratulations, and one of the Kreindlers who owned the expensive restaurant remarked: "Abe, with a show like this, you can afford to eat here."

The critics' notices were raves, apart from a few minor quibbles about the jocular treatment given the Mission members. The newspaper scribes appeared to be in competition over their various enthusiasms. Richard Watts was confident that Runyon would have been pleased by the show. "*Guys and Dolls* is just what it should be to celebrate the Runyon spirit, vigorous, noisy, humorous, tough on the surface and shamelessly sentimental underneath, filled with the salty characters and richly original language sacred to the memory of the Master, and a pleasure to all beholders." Just as he had assured Burrows, his colleague Brooks Atkinson concurred: though noting that the raffish, unbuttoned manners of Runyon's gangsters were toned down a bit for the times, he found *Guys and Dolls* to be "a work of art, gutsy and uproarious." "*Guys and Dolls* brings Broadway in off the street so you can see and hear it sitting down," proclaimed William Hawkins in the *New York World-Telegram and The Sun*, while John McClain of the *Journal American* called it the best thing since *Pal Joey*, and urged readers: "Run, don't walk, to the nearest ticket broker." John Chapman had one regret in the *Daily News*: "The big trouble with *Guys and Dolls* is that a performance of it lasts only one evening, when it ought to last about a week." Robert Coleman said in the *Mirror*: "Cy Feuer and Ernest Martin brought a musical champ to the 46th Street Theatre last night. It had everything, as a top-flight stake runner should." And George Jean Nathan, hailed as the foremost American theatre critic of the day, deemed the show a "fresh, humorous delight," though, astonishingly, he had cavils about the music, the "tedious opening dance number," and even the sets of Mielziner. Nathan thought that the remarkable quality was that "out of the vulgar low-life materials," the show managed "an evening devoid of all vulgarity in the common theatrical sense of the term and, further, without any of the cheapness and grossness that might ordinarily have been expected. It is, in fact, a show almost as innocent in its way as *Peter Pan*." Waxing on his subject, he went on: "Obedient to Runyon, it nevertheless has embellishments of its independent own, and some of them are equally inventive and funny. The most comical of the lines are always in character; there are none of the jokes, if we except such as a woman's studying a lengthy, expensive restaurant menu and then ordering a ham sandwich, that under less skilled and honest hands would have been dragged in as 'yaks'; and the general stage business, under George S. Kaufman's direction, is wittily maneuvered."

Everyone agreed that one of the greatest assets was the perfect casting. All the tinhorns and toughies got their due: "They would lift the fillings out of your teeth by chicanery or at the point of a gun. They're not exactly the type you'd invite to your home for an evening of sociable bridge. But you can't help liking the lot of them, because they have hearts to match their larcenous instincts." (Robert Coleman) As for the leads, there were great soundings of trumpet and drum: "Robert Alda is a superlative Sky Masterson. He's slick, handsome and persuasive. When he sings, it's like a lug and not a trained Met tenor." (Coleman) "Miss Bigley is the mission lass, and I had a funny feeling last night that she might never again learn a song that hadn't been specifically written for her." (William Hawkins) "Sam Levene is a backbone of wistful bravado and harrassed fence straddling, as the maestro of the meandering dotted cubes. He is so real, wearing his brave face, that he makes Broadway seem closer than down the block." (Hawkins) "[Vivian] Blaine...plays the soft-hard hot spot singer to the full, educated satisfaction of students of after-dark metropolitan animal life." (Nathan)

The show had a long run of 1,200 performances. With its 726th performance, it became the longest-running show in the history of the 46th Theatre, breaking the record held previously by Finian's Rainbow. Its operating profit was $10,100 a week, and after a year's run, the show earned a $510,000 profit on its $250,000 investment. Besides the resounding clatter of coins was the shower of distinctions and awards. John Chapman selected Guys and Dolls for inclusion in The Best Plays of 1950-1951 because of "its originality and its avoidance of the usual musical comedy pattern. In addition to winning the Outer Circle Critics' Award and The Aegis Theater Club Award, it won the New York Drama Critics' Circle Award as best musical (its most serious competition was The King and I, which it outpolled by a two-to-one margin). It also won the Donaldson Award, where Vivian Blaine, Robert Alda, Abe Burrows, Frank Loesser were also winners, and it swept the Tonys in the musical category, making off with Best Actor (Alda), Supporting Actress (Bigley), Director, Producers, Book, Composer and Lyricist, Choreographer, and Musical.

It was inevitable that England would get a version of the hit, for Damon Runyon was as popular there as in the States. Feuer and Martin asked Burrows to direct the 1953 British production, but because of the delay in the opening of Can-Can for which Burrows did the libretto, Art Lewis was invited to get the show on its feet with a mixed company of American and English actors. The producers would have preferred more Americans than they were permitted by British Equity, because the New York street textures and tones would ordinarily prove too difficult for the Brits. As it was, British Equity allowed five of the original American company—Vivian Blaine, Sam Levene, Stubby Kaye, Johnny Silver, and Tom Pedi—in addition to an American member of the British actors' union, Jerry Wayne.

Auditions were decidedly comic as British hopefuls put on weird versions of southern hillbilly or cowboy drawls ("I do American" was their clamouring assurance), and generally appeared to have derived their American accents from television shows. Fortunately, there were a couple of Canadians (including Lou Jacobi) who could do convincing "New Yorkese."The one Brit whose English style of speaking didn't seem incongruous with her role, was Lizbeth Webb who played Sarah.

The Coliseum was booked for the run of the show, but was unavailable for rehearsals which were then held in the chilly Drury Lane Theatre, where Nell Gwyn had once sold oranges. A large space with a very deep stage, it was home to a production of South Pacific, but the scenery for Guys and Dolls was erected behind the backdrop for the Rodgers and Hammerstein hit. After a week's tryout at the Hippodrome Theatre in Bristol, the production made its official London début on May 28. It was a success, marred only by one highly unpleasant incident near the end, when a group of anti-American rowdies high up in the gallery booed Vivian Blaine at her final bow. Others in the auditorium shouted back at the rowdies and applauded Blaine, sending the theatre into another uproar. The incident caused Kenneth Tynan to rush backstage to Vivian Blaine's dressing room and make apologies on behalf of the nation.

In his newspaper review, Tynan would seek to make further amends, if more than a little unfairly: "Miss Vivian Blaine (Miss Adelaide) is a very choice blonde judy and she gets to sing a song which goes as follows: 'Take back your mink to from whence it came' and which hits me slap-dad in the ear as being supernaturally comical. Myself, I prefer her to Miss

Lizbeth Webb, who plays the mission doll, but, naturally, I do not mention such an idea out loud." His admiring parody of the Runyon style concluded with the confession: "Personally, I found myself laughing ha-ha last night more often than a guy in the critical dodge has any right to. And I am ready to up and drop on my knees before Frank Loesser, who writes the music and lyrics. In fact, this Loesser is maybe the best light composer in the world. In fact, the chances are that *Guys and Dolls* is not only a young masterpiece, but the Beggar's Opera of Broadway."

Beginning with Tynan's, the English reviews were excellent, with *Punch* declaring: "It is difficult to know where to stop praising the clockwork precision of Mr. George S. Kaufman's production—certainly not before one has saluted the crap-shooting ballet from which the gyrating tinhorns emerge as deservedly deadbeat as from a University Boat Race: or to stop praising the brilliant settings of Mr. Jo Mielziner, or the astonishing costumes of Mr. Alvin Colt." *Variety's* London reviewer praised Arthur Lewis for his painstaking attention to detail, and gave him credit for "welding the British and American components into a smooth, forceful and spirited production which is distinguished by its vigorous presentation."

The sole exception to the chorus of praise was a critic who objected to the salaciousness of taking "a young Missionary girl to the edge of fornication." When Burrows was asked by a reporter what he thought of this remark, he cracked: "The fact is that the *edge* of fornication is a very safe place if you remain there."

The show lasted a year in London, and the cast had to give a Command Performance of "Sit Down, You're Rockin' the Boat" for the Royal Family. When Burrows was introduced to the Queen, he shook with nerves and homesickness as he thought of the Bronx and hotdogs.

The next reincarnation of the musical was the MGM movie version in 1955. Paramount had first-refusal rights but passed on them because Abe Burrows was on its studio blacklist—a legacy of Hollywood's notorious complicity with McCarthyism. When the Dramatists Guild opened bidding for the property, Sam Goldwyn prevailed with his offer of $1 million plus ten per cent of the gross. Burrows admired Goldwyn as "a bright, tough guy with a great love for films. And he made only films he personally liked." Goldwyn was famous for his malapropisms, which extended to curious twists in titles and names. Once, at the Burrows home for dinner, he told the host he had to leave early because he was to see Mary Martin and Ezio Pinza in Rodgers and Hammerstein's new hit, *Southern Pacific*. He called Marilyn Monroe "Marlene Monroe," and surprised Burrows by referring to "Sky Madison" instead of Sky Masterson.

After buying *Guys and Dolls*, Goldwyn visited Burrows in New York several times to discuss his screen treatment. At a particularly mellow meeting, he addressed Burrows' wife: "Carin, I am going to do the picture just the way this boy [pointing to Abe] wrote it. Sky Madison is going to be just as he was in the play, and so is Nathan Detroit." "That's wonderful, Sam. I hope you'll use Sam Levene." Goldwyn retorted sharply: "No, I don't want him to be Jewish." Which was especially curious, as Goldwyn was Jewish himself. What he really meant was that he wanted a star to play the part. Frank Sinatra was hired to do Nathan his way.

The movie *Guys and Dolls* had other surprises. Having spent $1 million on rights, Goldwyn poured in a further $4,500,000 on the production, most of this going to the stars. Burrows didn't write the screenplay; instead, Goldwyn hired Joseph L. Mankiewicz to do this, while Burrows was signed by another studio to the script for *The Solid Gold Cadillac*, a play by Kaufman and Howard Teichmann. The movie casting was odd in several instances: besides the crooning, sexy Sinatra incongruously cast as Nathan, there was pretty but non-musical Jean Simmons attempting straitlaced Sarah Brown, and husky, dramatic Marlon Brando cast as roguish Sky. Told of Brando's role, Harry Cohn of Columbia Pictures remarked: "Good for Goldwyn, bad for the picture." The Hot Box dancers were turned into The Alleycats, glamorous Goldwyn girls, whose first number showed an excessive amount of leg in a characteristic studio number. Almost needless to say, they had a Hollywood tackiness rather than a New York vaudevillian one. Five songs were cut, and Frank Loesser was recruited to write three new ones, "Adelaide," "Woman in Love," and "Pet Me, Poppa." Given his celebrity as a singer, Sinatra had to have additional songs, and although Loesser reluctantly agreed to this development, he chafed at his loss of artistic control. As Sinatra put his stamp on the songs, which consequently lost the sense of Nathan's brassy Broadway toughness, Loesser struggled to maintain his restraint. Of course, such restraint was bound to snap eventually.

After a rehearsal of "Sue Me" had practically given him an aneurysm, Loesser approached Sinatra to offer helpful tips on what he'd had in mind when he wrote the song. The offer was made through clenched teeth, and Sinatra responded coldly: "If you want to see me, you can come to my dressing room." Loesser left the set for a private spasm of jumping up and down and screaming his head off, then showed up at the star's dressing room which was crowded with hangers-on. Radio music blared. Loesser glared at Sinatra: "How the hell can we rehearse in this atmosphere?" "We'll do it my way, or you can fuck off." The only music that ensued was "a contrapuntal duet of explosions," (in Susan Loesser's words) "culminating in each man's avowal never to work with the other again." In the end, writes Susan Loesser, "Sinatra sang the song his way, my father refused to see the movie, and the two men never spoke to each other again."

For diehard Runyon fans and Broadway specialists, the movie was a wreck, its main attractions being Stubby Kaye (particularly in his unmatched "Sit Down, You're Rocking The Boat" number), the adenoidal Vivian Blaine, and Michael Kidd's spirited choreography.

Pauline Kael's review was harsh: "The Broadway version is legendary; the movie provides no clue why." Where others felt that director-scenarist Mankiewicz had tainted Burrows' book, she criticized him for seeming "to have fallen in love with Damon Runyon's cute, stilted locutions; the camera stands still while the actors mince through lines like 'This is no way for a gentleman to act and could lead to irritation on the part of Harry the Horse.'" Kael delivered a *coup de grâce*, calling the film "extended and rather tedious."

Given its male leads and the Cinemascope, Eastmancolor treatment, the movie couldn't but lose the convivial intimacy of the stage presentation, but, in truth, it had its curiously entertaining features—almost by default. Simmons, a fine screen actress of surprising versatility, was very funny in Sarah's Havana interlude, as she combined comic inebriation and sultriness. However, her dubbed voice didn't match her speaking pitch. Sinatra, of course, was Sinatra rather than Nathan Detroit, singing too well for the part through which he sauntered (as Clive Hirschhorn put it) "with the air of a lovable heel." Michael Freedland comments that where Sam Levene was as "tailor-made for the part as his suits had been for his body," Sinatra looked as if "he had got his clothes off-the-peg from a charity shop. Nathan was Jewish, Frank manifestly was not. Sam Levine [*sic*] was great in wide-shouldered chalk-stripes, Sinatra looked as though he still had a hanger in his jacket. Levine saying, 'So noo, so sue...call a policeman and sue me,' was right up his Brooklyn street. Sinatra seemed as though he had got lost on the journey from Hoboken and was with a crowd of people he didn't know very well." Years later, Sinatra would admit that Nathan was "the only part I was ever very disappointed with." He claimed to have been pressured into playing it and that he had really wanted the part of Sky Masterson. "I mean nothing disparaging about Marlon Brando, but Masterson didn't fit him and he knew it."

In fact, Brando was a mixed delight. While his singing was too weak for the leading part—a reviewer likened it to "the mating call of a yak"—and his acting sometimes sullen and gloomy, he managed a crude innocence and an occasional roguish charm. Given the overall lack of stylized coherence, he could not be blamed for the "arty" stiltedness of his "Luck Be A Lady" number. Pauline Kael found him and Simmons to be "ingratiatingly uneasy when they burst into song and dance."

In his autobiography, *Brando: Songs My Mother Taught Me*, the actor described the tortuous processes of editing, splicing, and lip-synching that finally produced his film sound: after a few weeks with an Italian singing coach, Brando had to record his songs in a studio so that they could then be synchronized with shots of him mouthing the words on film. "I couldn't hit a note in the dubbing room with a baseball bat; some notes I missed by extraordinary margins. But the engineers kept telling me to do them over and over again, and they would stitch together a word here, a note there, until they had a recording that sounded like I'd sung the bars consecutively. They sewed my words together in one song so tightly that when I mouthed it in front of the camera, I nearly asphyxiated myself because I couldn't breathe while trying to synchronize my lips."

But Hollywood musicals are a species all their own, and the radically flawed Goldwyn movie (which was a box-office hit) couldn't obliterate memories of its Broadway source. Fortunately, a cast recording of the original show was waxed (issued first on the Brunswick label, but best known by the Decca DL 8036 listing), and this not only preserves a sense of the sound of that classic, it remains (as Kurt Gänzl claims) "one of the most outstanding achievements in the musical theatre." The recording showed that the score had everything: a Runyonland introduction (magnificently orchestrated by George Bassman and Ted Royal), a fugue for tinhorns, sweeping melodies, cabaret novelties, scalding counterpoints and harmonies, and gospel numbers. Kurt Gänzl's concise comments deserve quotation: "Adelaide (Vivian Blaine) hammers out 'A Bushel and a Peck' in a voice to rival Merman's, but wholly convincing you that she is this seedy cabaret singer before lapsing into the sniffles and stentorian miseries of her Lament. By the time you get to the second part of the second side...you are wallowing in just about the nearest thing to perfection...Even the little piece 'More I Cannot Wish You,' which can slip away ineffectively in a less than well cast production, is given an exquisite performance here by veteran Pat Rooney sr., whose gentle, crackly Irish tones take the sugar off its sweet sentiments." Gänzl rightly concluded that this recording was essential to a true collector.

Having been recognized as a classic in its own time, Guys and Dolls submits to frequent revivals, despite the current era's fondness for mega-musicals and the whole panoply of technical elaboration—miking, synthesizers, extravagant scenic décor, and special visual effects. The show remains refreshingly old-fashioned, blissfully free of mechanical contraptions that would exhaust rather than lift its spirit. Time has not eroded its virtues (the greatest of which are its libretto and music) the way changing fashion has lessened the appeal of most Rodgers and Hammerstein shows or Irving Berlin musicals. Its verbal and musical idioms are an indelible signature of Broadway, "as much a part of [the American] landscape as the Chrysler Building and Radio City Music Hall" (in Frank Rich's phrase).

The thing about classics is that they invite re-imaginings, and the special challenge in this case is for theatre artists to find an approach that is different from the 1950 version while being at least equally as exciting. This does not mean, however, allowing the moral climate of the times to dictate the tone. *Guys and Dolls* is not an innocent pastime for those bent on family values; but neither is it a licentious parable of a compulsive gambler and a nightclub singer who have sex without benefit of marriage. But how to capture a larger-than-life idiom with the heat, light, and freneticism that echoes the neon-hued tumult of the Times Square that spawned it, while testing the piece against the temper of a new time?

Revivals have come to define modern Broadway, their peak probably reached in the seventies. In the 1975-76 season, there were 28 revivals of various shows; in the next, 17. In most instances, the musical revivals were characterized by a common purpose: the recapturing of the exact thrust and glamour of the original productions. *Porgy and Bess* was done in a seldom-seen original, uncut version. *The King and I* remained the royal prerogative of Yul Brynner all through his lifetime. And despite the various interpretations of Tevye by the like of Zero Mostel, Topol, and Herschel Bernardi, *Fiddler on the Roof* was always mounted under the auspices of Jerome Robbins' original conception.

The most radical reinterpretation of *Guys and Dolls* came in 1976 with an all-black cast that cut to the heart of its sociology. Damon Runyon's Broadway is definably white (it is all cheesecake or strudel, and its hoodlums dress in pinstripes), but it is undeniably urban. Times Square today is quite different from that of Runyon's day, and the colours and tones of the landscape are richly varied. So, it was inevitable that a black company could itself act as a re-interpretation of *Guys and Dolls*, as Mel Gussow pointed out in his review of the 1976 production. "Mindy's cheesecake is now apple pie and ice-cream. Adelaide retains her nasality, but, being black, loses her New York accent. The new tone is accentuated in performance in the dancing, walking, singing, and talking (greeters slap

hands)." Putting aside the flaws of flimsy sets and sparse choreography, Gussow noted the "black" assets: the funkiness of
Ernestine Jackson's rendition of "If I Were A Bell;" the Duke
Ellington accents in James Randolph's version of "My Time of
Day;" Robert Guillaume's "deadpan and offhanded" Nathan,
"somewhat in the manner of Bill Cosby;" and Ken Page's Nicely-
Nicely that turned "Sit Down" into a hand-clapping, tambourine-slapping gospel song, "a soul-stopper (two deserved encores on opening night) that almost obliterates the memory
of the seemingly unforgettable Stubby Kaye in the original 1950
Broadway production."

Not everyone was as enchanted as Gussow, however, when
Harlem so strongly infiltrated white Manhattan. Despite the
show's three Tony nominations (including one for Most Innovative Production of a Revival), Kurt Gänzl was notably disapproving of the whooped-up staging when he complained:
"Loesser's score underwent the sort of treatment only a dead
writer could suffer in silence as his music was twisted about
into corny upbeat arrangements by Messers Danny Holgate
and Horace Ott and his lyrics 'improved' by someone who
doesn't own up on the record sleeve." Allowing for a certain
degree of conservatism in Gänzl's response, the fact remains
that the all-black Guys and Dolls changed the atmosphere and
tone of the Burrows-Loesser original, though with far more
point than would be possible for an all-white Porgy and Bess.

A classic, especially a musical one, transcends questions of
race and nationality, though when the English re-interpret a
Broadway classic, there is understandable anxiety about their
accents and approach. The English tend to be more reticent
than Americans in their singing and acting, and their choreography is usually less rambunctious and innovative than their
American counterpart—as was most recently demonstrated
in Simon Callow's rather lame 1999 Toronto mounting of The
Pajama Game. When the English use songbook formats (as in

Cowardy Custard, Cole, and Side by Side by Sondheim) or class-con-
scious period settings (as in My Fair Lady, Les Misérables, or A Little
Night Music), their work is fluent and impressive. Notwithstand-
ing the ascent of Andrew Lloyd Webber and his flamboyant,
operatic creations, the English scale is generally narrow and
small. Yet, their awe for the Broadway musical draws the
English irresistibly to revivals of Broadway classics.

In the musical theatre genre, there is no English snobbery.
From the late, lamented Lord Olivier to the phenomenal Dame
Judi Dench, from the swanlike Natasha Richardson to the
rough-hewn Bob Hoskins, English performers can all be cap-
tives of Broadway musicals. In fact, some of the most intrigu-
ing re-interpretations of Broadway classics have come through
the directorial genius of young Englishmen such as Nicholas
Hytner (Carousel) and Sam Mendes (Cabaret), although there is
no question that the English continue to blur their choreography and mess up their American accents. Even the best English
production of Guys and Dolls, done at the Royal National Theatre
in 1982, under the direction of Richard Eyre, suffered in at
least one area, with Sheridan Morley's calling the casting "brave
to foolhardy."

The ghost of Olivier hovered over that production. In the
closing years of his tenure as the National's first Artistic Director, Olivier had dreamed of doing the musical. His Literary
Manager, Kenneth Tynan, had given him the idea, calling Guys
and Dolls "the second best American play" (the best being Death
of a Salesman). Olivier had invited his friend Garson Kanin to
come over from New York to direct. Kanin, for his part, brought
over an acrobatic dancer to teach the English cast the song and
dance numbers. The stage boards had resounded with the tap-
ping of feet as Geraldine McEwan as Adelaide, Dennis Quilley
as Sky, and Louise Purnell as Sarah practised their numbers,
and did voice lessons, particularly on hard consonants, to get
their American accents right. McEwan observed as Oliver re-

hearsed his role of Nathan Detroit: "It was so sort of tired and casual and laid-back. Oh, I don't know, it was very shrugged off, the way he played it. He would have been wonderful."

However, illness and a board of directors intervened. An embolism in a leg put Olivier in hospital and out of the board rooms where a unilateral decision was made to cancel the production. What particularly stung Olivier was the treachery of his supposed friend "Binkie" Beaumont, who was reported to have said: "I wouldn't have objected if the proposed musical had been *Oklahoma!*" It was so infuriatingly daft as to be immortal: the astonishing thought of Olivier as a dancing cowboy would have certainly brought in the crowds, but the corn would really have been as high as an elephant's eye.

When Richard Eyre joined the National as Associate Director in mid 1981, and was asked by Peter Hall, Olivier's successor, to think of staging a "major popular classic," he settled on *Guys and Dolls*, aware of the irony of mounting it in the theatre bearing Olivier's name.

Eyre had come to the musical through his father's overcoat—a "loudish belted check coat with giant shoulder" and nicknamed Big Nig. Then twelve years old, he had asked his father: "Why is your coat called Big Nig?" "Read more than somewhat and you'll find out," came the reply. The boy was puzzled: his eyes already ached from his habit of reading more than somewhat by torchlight under the bedcovers. "'More Than Somewhat'!" his father growled, "by Damon Runyon."

Taking up the story, he discovered that Big Nig was a crapshooter and Runyon a unique writer.

Eyre saw the 1955 MGM movie, and though entertained by Brando and Simmons, was not that pleased by Sinatra's Nathan. A view that was to be shared by Bob Hoskins who was to play the same role with rich vulgarity.

Eyre had three months to cast, design, and plan. He had directed musicals before, but never on this scale. With the budget pointed at £94,000, he and designer John Gunter started work in mid-October. The pair realized that their design choices were limited to two options: either "a standing set that would embrace all locations, and a production that laid little emphasis on the old fashioned production values of the Broadway musical," or "to go for broke—epic, spectacular, extrovert and flamboyant. Broadway as we imagined it in its heyday." Eyre and Gunter discussed Hollywood films: gangster movies and their visual hallmarks, Gene Kelly musicals that blended studio naturalism with extreme fantasy, Martin Scorsese's *New York, New York* that was lurid with affectation, parody, and bravura. After discussing how each scene of the show could be filmed, they then wondered how to translate it appropriately on the large Olivier stage. The National would not sponsor a "research" trip to New York, so the pair drew heavily on Andreas Feininger's photographs of New York in the forties. As Gunter devised a structure to suggest Times Square by day, Eyre and he struggled over its representation at night. They thought of neon, but felt it would be too bright and impractical—until Eyre came upon Rudi Stern's *Let There Be Neon* in a Paris booksop one weekend. "Neon is writing with light," Stern said, and this became the designer's cue to transform the stage space, to move fluently and elegantly from the large-scale to the intimate while making each location real and specific.

Production ideas came in brainstorms. At one point it was thought that the Havana cafe scene should have only émigrés from films set in Cuba—Humphrey Bogart, Lauren Bacall, Carmen Miranda, Sydney Greenstreet, and, perhaps, Fidel Castro. The production team eventually settled for a drag queen and an eccentric local clientele.

Casting made it clear that this production had a charmed life. Bob Hoskins was a croaky-voiced Nathan with an East End Method style; Julia McKenzie, with considerable experience in musicals, was nasal-toned Adelaide. Ian Charleson played Sky; Julie Covington, who had performed Tom Stoppard and David Hare, was Sarah. Eyre was delighted that all the actors he wanted for the show were available to him. "'We want people with bumps,' said Cy Feuer of the original Guys and Dolls production. Our cast was richly corrugated." The seven-week rehearsal period began with tap lessons for the cast and repetitive song and dance harmonies. Eyre wanted the show to end "with the entire cast tap dancing down Broadway," so it was incumbent on choreographer David Toguri to dispel all fears about non-rhythmic Brits. While a professional croupier taught them crap-shooting, Toguri worked assiduously on the dances. "David made people who couldn't move, move," said Sue Blane, costume designer. "He focused on the ones who could dance, and it's all to his credit that the finalé was such a treat."

Kevin Williams, the Rusty Charley of the show, realized Toguri's contribution: "Besides the Hat Box dancers [sic], only Julia, Bernard Sharpe [Hot Horse Herbie] and myself had training. The basic problem is rhythm—I don't think Brits are born with it! There were workshops every morning and the choreographer worked with the actors, keeping the rhythm basic and then alternating with more experienced dancers to create a nice ensemble effect. It does wonders to see twenty-six people doing the same steps at a time."

"We rehearsed like a play," Eyre commented. "It really was an outstanding group of actors; their singing was quite musical and there was a real sense of energy. It wasn't regimented."

Eyre would not allow his cast to descend to parody. He wanted truthfulness, pointing out that "Runyon's world is as hermetic, consistent and original as P.G. Wodehouse's and must be played for real if its spell is to work." He insisted that the cast familiarize themselves with the Runyon stories to find out who and what their characters were. The result was an enviably high degree of individualization: no character could be mistaken for another.

Sue Blane's costumes helped in the matter. Her clothes were concocted from ideas out of old American movies and tacky Frederick of Hollywood catalogues. "The wonderful thing about *Guys and Dolls* is that you can vulgarize it, especially Miss Adelaide and her dancers. When you work with period clothes, it's helpful for the focus of the character, to give people helpful information and pointers on how to feel. You can't use real clothes because they're too detailed and faded and don't fit perfectly." Blane consulted the cast about their costumes and showed them drawings first. It was difficult to get anything in a broad pin-stripe for Bob Hoskins, so his suit was made of "the inside-out-side of Italian suiting." On its hanger, the suit was completely square in shape, but it was wonderfully appropriate to Hoskins' physique and characterization. Hoskins' costume was crowned by a wide-brimmed hat for his first two scenes. He'd come off the stage, swearing that he couldn't see, but he had to wear it in order to establish Nathan's character early on.

Cast and crew were proud of the show. It was a very close company, but the real fun didn't begin until the technical run-through. "We all knew there was something exciting and the buzzing went on all week," remembers Blane. Kevin Williams adds: "*Guys and Dolls* was probably the biggest party ever held on stage. It was the ultimate fusion of a near-perfect company."

But it was not until the first preview that everyone knew they had a palpable hit with audiences. "Sit Down, You're Rocking the Boat" stopped the show cold, and even the built-in, choreographed reprise was not enough for the audience that simply refused to let the show go on. Bob Hoskins had to confer hastily with the musical director to get cast and orchestra back together in unison at the right cue. The official first night was so charged with electric excitement that the audience almost felt the floor lifting beneath their feet. Peter Lewis, chronicler of the National's history, wrote: "Even when you stepped outside, slightly dazed, into the night, the pavement had an unaccountable spring to it."

The vast majority of London critics agreed, when the production officially opened March 9, 1982, with Milton Shumlin in the *Standard* doubting if in its career the National Theatre had ever given the audience "such unalloyed pleasure." Unlike the first British production, this one didn't mix Americans with Brits. Indeed, it was all-English from top to bottom, and a real National achievement, although Sheridan Morley had reservations in *Punch* about the four principals, finding Hoskins "more Hammersmith than New York Broadway," McKenzie "patently too great and good a singer ever to have been confined to the crummy Hot Box nightclub," Ian Charleson "years too young and innocent," and Julie Covington oddly lacking "the requisite Major Barbara fervour." These cavils aside, Morley's overall verdict was highly favourable: "From its filmic opening titles, which sensibly haul the memory back into the Warner Brothers' black-and-white 1940s from the false Goldwyn Technicolor image of Brando and Sinatra, right through to John Normington doing 'More I Cannot Wish You' quite beautifully, this is a production in which the whole is always greater than its parts. It is a tapestry of small-time losers and big-band numbers, and...it manages to fill the Olivier stage with the brassy sound and tacky soul of Runyon's Broadway."

But the ultimate judges of Broadway musicals are Americans themselves for they know the form and history better than anyone else. While there were some critics (such as Kurt Gänzl) who found the English production wanting in several key areas, there were others who were pleasantly surprised. Gänzl, of course, reviewed the cast album, not the "live" production, but he nevertheless complained bitterly of the atrocious arrangements and some of the singing: "Several of the principal performers sound very uncomfortable in their singing and only the assured Julia McKenzie (Adelaide), galloping into her cabaret numbers with abandon and ending her cavalcade of woes with a sneeze at Yma Sumac level, and David Healy (Nicely-Nicely), with a lusty 'Sit Down You're Rockin' the Boat,' make the grade." But in *Broadway Babies*, Ethan Mordden offered a contrary view to Gänzl's disapproval: "Chrysalis recorded it, American accents and all (not a single slip), with brassy orchestrations respectful of the originals. It's a more complete reading, and this team is far superior to the home squad, especially the Adelaide, Julia McKenzie." Enough to make us wonder whether Gänzl and Mordden had listened to the same recording.

The real test of any new version of *Guys and Dolls*, beyond the obvious one of the sound of the show, is whether director and cast recognize that romance is built into the very text. As Frank Rich noted in his review of the 1992 Broadway revival, under Jerry Zaks' direction, Runyon didn't reach Manhattan until he was twenty-six, so his love for his adopted town was "the helplessly romantic ardor of a pilgrim who finally found his Mecca." That romance is one "in which the hoods and chorus girls engage in no violence, never mention sex, and speak in an exaggeratedly polite argot that is as courtly as dese-and-dose vernacular can be."

Zaks' production redefined Broadway dazzle. Assisted immeasurably by an extraordinary design team led by Tony Walton, and a cast that maintained a fast pace while hitting all the notes for comedy and emotion, *Guys and Dolls* consolidated its fame as a tough-talking, big-hearted musical. The sour, cynical center of the libretto was faithfully preserved despite the Broadway high jinks. Overall, there was an unmistakable sense that the glory went beyond nostalgia, though Walton's painted drops reconjured the Broadway design mechanics of the fifties. His black-and-white front curtain of an urban scene went up to reveal the same scene, now painted on a backdrop, that remade New York in the deeply saturated colours of Matisse and Dufy. Building on the cherished imagery of Jo Mielziner, Walton also incorporated memories of Edward Hopper's New York, while enticing audiences to see the show anew. A similar refreshening of the past occurred in William Ivey Long's costumes which paid a debt to Alvin Colt and Irene Sharaff, while exercising their new boldness and extravagant iridescence. As for the lighting, Paul Gallo, who had recently rendered a glittery old Times Square in Crazy For You, presented rich hues that would have been envied by other designers in the days of Loesser and Burrows. He painted New York as a nocturnal paradise spelled out in large, blinking signs. A New York romanticized to the point of fantasy, yet true to the spirit of Loesser's lyric that has a "street lamp light fill[ing] the gutter with gold."

So, nothing in the revival imprisoned the show in the past. Even Christopher Chadman's choreography (that was in the spirit of Michael Kidd's original) and the orchestrations of Michael Starobin and Michael Gibson showed no anxiety of early influences. As for the casting, though Nathan Lane was hardly in the vein of Sam Levene, his Nathan Detroit became increasingly ingratiating. Lane discovered subtextual clues about Nathan, and in the "Sue Me" number, usually done as a throwaway, he and his director found something dramatic. Lane revealed a Nathan sincerely struggling to convince Adelaide that he loved her, and his modulations into tenderness and affection were heartwarming. Peter Gallagher's peculiar combination of rugged glamour and mellow singing tones turned Sky Masterson into a commanding presence, modulating from sly

shyness to gritty toughness, and from brooding to infatua-
tion. His Sarah, Josie de Guzman, helped make his sweet in-
fatuation credible by being bemusedly prim rather than puri-
tanically austere. Sharing her director's concept of the part as
"a real healer—someone who's good at what she does but is
in the wrong place," Guzman played Sarah as a "doll" who
was ready to blossom in her other self but hadn't found the
right person yet.

Walter Bobbie's Nicely-Nicely, far thinner than his stage
predecessors (and therefore true to Runyon's original), led
"Sit Down, You're Rockin' the Boat" to a spectacular frenzy,
managing to break free of the Stubby Kaye imprint. His gangster cohorts—J.K. Simmons (Benny Southstreet), Ernie Sabella
(Harry the Horse), and Herschel Sparber (Big Jule)—had the
requisite mugs without being carbon copies of their 1950
prototypes.

But the biggest, freshest reinterpretation came in the deftly
comic performance of Faith Prince as adenoidal Adelaide. Looking like a bracing cross between Judy Holliday and Vivian Blaine,
Prince stopped the show with her sneeze-laden lament in Act
1, and then again in Act 2 where she executed the stripteasing
"Take Back Your Mink" as "one long nasal kvetch." (Rich) Larger
in stature than Blaine, and made all the bigger with piled blond
hair, Prince was part squeaky Marilyn Monroe, part prema-
ture, roaring matron. Hers was a legendary musical comedy
creation that showed, as the production itself did, that a new
Broadway generation can find a different, exciting way to
reimagine a classic.

# PRODUCTION NOTES

GUYS AND DOLLS WAS FIRST PRESENTED by Cy Feuer and Ernest Martin at the Forty-Sixth Street Theatre, New York, on November 24, 1950. The cast was as follows:

| | |
|---|---|
| Nicely-Nicely Johnson | *Stubby Kayne* |
| Benny Southstreet | *Johnny Silver* |
| Rusty Charlie | *Douglas Deane* |
| Sarah Brown | *Isabel Bigley* |
| Arvide Abernathy | *Pat Rooney, Sr.* |
| Mission Band | *Margery Oldroyd, Paul Migan, Christine Matsios* |
| Harry the Horse | *Tom Pedi* |
| Lt. Brannigan | *Paul Reed* |
| Nathan Detroit | *Sam Levene* |
| Angie the Ox | *Tony Gardell* |
| Miss Adelaide | *Vivian Blaine* |
| Sky Masterson | *Robert Alda* |
| Joey Biltmore | *Bern Hoffman* |
| Mimi | *Beverly Tassoni* |
| General Matilda B. Cartwright | *Netta Packer* |
| Big Jule | *B.S. Pully* |
| Drunk | *Eddie Phillips* |
| Waiter | *Joe Milan* |

Dancers: *Wana Allison, Geraldine Delaney, Barbara Ferguson, Lee Joyce, Marcia Maier, Beverly Tassoni, Ruth Vernon, Onna White, Forrest Bonshire, Peter Gennaro, Joe Milan, Eddie Phillips, Harry Lee Rogers, Bud Schwab, Merritt Thompson*

Singers: *Beverly Lawrence, Christine Matsios, Charles Drake, Tony Gardell, Bern Hoffman, Carl Nicholas, Don Russell, Hal Saunders, Earle Styres*

Based on a Story and Characters by *Damon Runyon*
Music and Lyrics by *Frank Loesser*
Book by *Jo Swerling and Abe Burrows*
Dances and Musical Numbers by *Michael Kidd*
Settings and Lighting by *Jo Mielziner*
Costumes by *Alvin Colt*
Musical Direction by *Irving Actman*
Orchestral Arrangements by *George Bassman and Ted Royal*
Vocal Arrangements and Direction by *Herbert Greene*
Staged by *George S. Kaufman*

# BIBLIOGRAPHY

Alpert, Hollis. *Broadway! (125 Years of Musical Theatre)*. New York: Arcade Publishing/Little, Brown, 1991.

Amberg, George. *Ballet: The Emergence of an American Art*. New York: Mentor, 1951.

Anderson, Doug. "Stubby Kaye: Show Stopper." *Theatre Arts* Feb. 1952, 39.

"At The Play." Review of *Guys and Dolls*. *Punch* 10 June 1953, 698.

Atkinson, Brooks. "At The Theatre." Rev. of *Guys and Dolls*. *New York Times* 25 Nov. 1950.

Barnes, Howard. "Brassy Broadway." *New York Herald Tribune* 25 Nov. 1950.

Barret, Dorothy. "The Designing Mr. Colt." *Dance* Nov. 1945, 14, 37.

Batelle, Phyllis. "Star in Search of Security." *New York Journal- American* 3 May 1958.

Beckerman, Bernard and Howard Siegman, eds. *On Stage. Selected Theater Reviews from The New York Times 1920-1970*. New York: Arno Press, 1973.

Bentley, Eric. "Comedy and the Comic Spirit in America." *What Is Theatre?* New York: Limelight Editions, 1984.

Bigley, Isabel. "White Lie Paid Off For Isabel Bigley." *New York World-Telegram and The Sun* 16 Aug. 1952.

Block, Geoffrey. *Enchanted Evenings (The Broadway Musical from 'Show Boat' to Sondheim)*. New York: Oxford University Press, 1997.

Bolton, Whitney. "Happy Occasion—Honoring Levene, Actor of Distinction." *New York Morning Telegraph* 17 Dec. 1962.

Bordman, Gerald. *American Musical Comedy: From 'Adonis' to 'Dreamgirls.'* New York: Oxford UP, 1982.
_____. *American Musical Theatre. (A Chronicle)*, 2nd ed. New York: Oxford UP, 1992.

Brando, Marlon (with Robert Lindsey). *Brando: Songs My Mother Taught Me*. Toronto: Random House, 1994.

Burrows, Abe. "Guys and Dolls." *Theatre Arts* July 1951, 30.
_____. *Honest, Abe*. Boston: Little, Brown and Co., 1980.
_____. "Humor Has Helped Mankind To Survive in Difficult Times." *The Daily Compass* (N.Y.) 21 Mar. 1950.
"Burrows Denies He Was Real Red." *New York Times* 13 Nov. 1952.

Brown, John Mason. *As They Appear*. New York: McGraw-Hill, 1952.
_____. "Nicely-Nicely." *The Saturday Review* 23 Dec. 1950, 27-28.

Carmer, Carl. "George S. Kaufman: Playmaker to Broadway." *Theatre Arts Monthly* Oct. 1932, 807-815.

Chapman, John. "'Guys and Dolls' New York's Own Musical Comedy—So Get in Line." *Daily News* 25 Nov. 1950.

Clark, Tom. *The World of Damon Runyon*. New York: Harper & Row, 1978.

———, ed. *The Bloodhounds of Broadway and other stories by Damon Runyon*. New York: William Morrow, 1981.

Coe, Richard L. "'Guys and Dolls' Is Smash for Loesser." *Washington Post* 17 Jan. 1951.

Coleman, Robert. "Runyon's 'Guys and Dolls' Proves Magnificent Hit." *Daily Mirror* 25 Nov. 1950.

"Colt's Costumes." *New Yorker* 6 Jan. 1951.

Cooke, Richard P. "Best in Two Seasons." *Wall Street Journal* 27 Nov. 1950.

Darlington, W.A. "London Report on 'Guys and Dolls.'" *New York Times* 7 June 1953.

Denby, Edwin. *Dance Writings*. Ed. by Robert Cornfield and William Mackay. New York: Alfred A. Knopf, 1986.

———. *Looking At The Dance*. New York: Popular Library, 1968.

D'Itri, Patricia Ward. *Damon Runyon*. Boston: Twayne, 1982.

"The Easygoing Method." Profile of Burrows. *New Yorker* 11 May 1957, 51-79.

Engel, Lehman. *Their Words Are Music: The Great Theatre Lyricists and their Lyrics*. New York: Crown Publishers, 1975.

———. *Words With Music: The Broadway Musical Libretto*. New York: Schirmer Books, 1981.

Ewen, David. *American Songwriters.* New York: The H.W. Wilson Co., 1987.

_____. *Complete Book of The American Musical Theatre.* (Rev.) New York: Henry Holt, 1959.

Freedland, Michael. *All The Way (A Biography of Frank Sinatra).* London: Orion, 1998.

Gänzl, Kurt. *The Blackwell Guide to the Musical Theatre on Record.* Oxford: Basil Blackwell, 1990.

Gary, Beverly. *"A Broadway Success Finds Gentleness Is The Soul of Wit."* *New York Post* 21 Nov. 1961.

Gilbert, Douglas. "George S. Kaufman's Wit Yielded Him Big Bank Balances—He Missed Being an Actor and Became Instead a Playwright." *New York World-Telegram* 11 June 1935.

Gottfried, Martin. *Broadway Musicals.* New York: Abradale Press/Harry N. Abrams, 1984.

Green, Stanley. *Encyclopedia of the Musical Theatre.* New York: Da Capo Press, 1976.

_____. *The World of Musical Comedy.* New York: Grosset & Dunlap, 1962.

Guernsey, Otis L., Jr., ed. *Broadway Song & Story. (Playwrights/Lyricists/Composers Discuss Their Hits).* New York: Dodd, Mead, 1985.

_____, ed. *Playwrights, Lyricists, Composers On Theater.* New York: Dodd, Mead, 1974.

Gussow, Mel. *Theatre On The Edge: New Visions, New Voices.* New York: Applause, 1998.

*The Guys and Dolls Book.* (Commemorating the National Theatre of Great Britain production.) London: Methuen, 1982.

Harris, Harry. "Brooklyn's Erudite Funnyman Hits Jackpot with 'Guys and Dolls.'" *Philadelphia Bulletin* 22 Oct. 1950.
_____. "Pat Rooney, 70, Still a Twinkletoes in Musical Here." *Philadelphia Evening Bulletin* 20 Oct. 1950.

Havemann, Ernest. "The Fine Art of the Hit Tune." *Life* 8 Dec.1952, 163-174.

Hawkins, William. "'Guys and Dolls'—Wow!" *NewYork World Telegram and The Sun* 25 Nov. 1950.

Hirschhorn, Clive. *The Hollywood Musical.* New York: Portland House, 1991.

Jackson, Arthur. *The Best Musicals: From 'Show Boat' to 'A ChorusLine'.* (Foreword by Clive Barnes.) New York: Crown, 1977.

Kael, Pauline. *5001 Nights at the Movies: A Guide from A to Z.* New York: Holt, Rinehart and Winston, 1982.

Kasha, Al and Joel Hirschhorn. *Notes on Broadway: Intimate Conversations with Broadway's Greatest Songwriters.* New York: A Fireside Book, 1987.

Keating, John. "Abe Burrows: Play Doctor." *Cue* 1 Mar. 1952, 10-11.

Kinnaird, Clark, ed. *A Treasury of Damon Runyon.* New York: The Modern Library, 1958.

Laufe, Abe. *Broadway's Greatest Musicals.* New York: Funk & Wagnalls, 1970.

Lerner, Alan Jay. *The Musical Theatre. A Celebration.* London: Collins, 1986.

Lewis, Emory. "GM's Dance Kidd." *Cue* 21 Jan. 1956, 18, 47.

Little, Stuart W. "Frank Loesser: Who Wants a Festival?" *New York Herald Tribune* 17 Apr. 1966.

Loesser, Susan. *A Most Remarkable Fella: Frank Loesser and the Guys and Dolls in his Life.* New York: Donald I. Fine, 1993.

McClain, John. "The Best Thing Since 'Pal Joey.'" *Journal American* 25 Nov. 1950.
_____. "'Guys and Dolls' Team Up To Make Broadway History." *Pictorial Review* 24 Dec. 1950, 14P.

McCrary, Tex and Jinx Falkenberg. "New York Close-Up." *New York Herald Tribune* 19 Feb. 1951.
_____. "New York Close-Up." *New York Herald Tribune* 17 Dec. 1950.

Meredith, Scott. *George S. Kaufman and his friends.* Garden City, New York: Doubleday, 1974.

Mielziner, Jo. *Designing for the Theatre: A Memoir And A Portfolio.* New York: Bramhall House, 1965.

Milstead, Janey. "Robert Alda: Cornerstone of a Three Generation Acting Family." *Soap Opera Digest* 15 Sept. 1981, 12-15, 126.

Mockridge, Norton. "Abe Burrows Proves No Half-Type Wit, Yet." *New York World-Telegram* 28 Oct. 1949.

Moline, Karen. *Bob Hoskins: An Unlikely Hero.* London: Sphere Books, Ltd., 1988.

Mordden, Ethan. *Better Foot Forward: The History of American Musical Theatre*. New York: Grossman/Viking, 1976.

_____. *Broadway Babies: The People Who Made the American Musical*. New York: Oxford UP, 1983.

_____. *Coming Up Roses (The Broadway Musical In The 1950s)*. New York/Oxford: Oxford University Press, 1998.

_____. *The Hollywood Musical*. New York: St. Martin's Press, 1981.

Morley, Sheridan. *Shooting Stars (Plays and Players 1975-1983)*. London: Quartet Books, 1983.

Morse, Arthur D. "The Doll in Guys and Dolls." [sic] *Collier's* 27 Jan. 1951, 26-27, 72-73.

Nathan, George Jean. "Guys and Dolls." *The Theatre Book of the Year (1950-1951). A Record and an Interpretation*. New York: Alfred A. Knopf, 1951.

Ormsbee, Helen. "How a Song Grew Into a Starring Role." *New York Herald Tribune* 28 Jan. 1951.

_____. "Isabel Bigley Puts Name in Lights." *New York Herald Tribune* 16 Sept. 1951.

"Out of the Parlor." *New Yorker* 6 Nov. 1948, 23-24.

"Past Master." *Time* 20 Nov. 1939.

P.K. "Kaye Has Played Nicely-Nicely Through Four Suits of Clothes." *San Francisco Chronicle* 8 Jan. 1956.

Rasky, Frank. "Guys & Dolls." *New Liberty* Mar. 1951, Vol. 28, No.1, 18-19, 83-86.

Rev. of *Guys and Dolls*. *Variety* 18 Oct. 1950.

Rev. of London production of *Guys and Dolls*. *Variety* 6 May 1953.

Rice, Vernon. "Alvin Colt Has a System For Handling Actresses." *New York Post* 29 Oct. 1947.

Rich, Frank. Hot Seat (*Theater Criticism for The New York Times, 1980-1993*). New York: Random House, 1998.

Runyon, Damon. *Runyon From First to Last.* (*containing all the stories written by Damon Runyon and not included in 'Runyon on Broadway'*). London: Constable, 1972.

"Sam Levene's Appearance in 'Guys and Dolls' Is His First Experience in a Musical Show." *Newark News* 2 Aug. 1952.

Schumach, Murray. "Frank Loesser—Hit Parade Habitué." *New York Times* 17 Dec. 1950.

Sheaffer, Louis. "Brooklyn Guy Named Burrows Talks Seriously About Humor." *Brooklyn Eagle* 2 Apr. 1951.

Stephens, Robert. *Knight Errant: Memoirs of a Vagabond Actor.* London: Sceptre, 1996.

Sullivan, Robert. "How To Bring In A Broadway Smash." *Sunday News* 24 Dec. 1950.

Suskin, Steven. *Opening Night on Broadway.* New York: Schirmer, 1990.

Swados, Elizabeth. *Listening Out Loud: Becoming a Composer.* New York: Perennial Library, 1989.

Swain, Joseph P. *The Broadway Musical: A Critical and Musical Survey.* New York: Oxford UP, 1990.

Swerling, Jo and Abe Burrows. *Guys and Dolls* (*A Musical Fable of Broadway*). From *the American Drama* (*The Modern Theatre Series Volume Four*), ed. Eric Bentley. Garden City, N.Y.: Doubleday Anchor Books, 1956.

Talley, Rhea. "Overlord of the Undieworld." *Courier-Journal Magazine* 1 Apr. 1951.

Tallmer, Jerry. "It Comes Out Funny." *New York Post* 28 Dec. 1965.

Taubman, Howard. *The Making of the American Theatre*. New York: Coward McCann, 1965.

Teichmann, Howard. *George S. Kaufman: An Intimate Portrait*. New York: Atheneum, 1972.

Watson, John. "Miss B. Breaks Adelaide's Spell." *New York Journal- American* 22 June 1958.

Watts, Richard, Jr. "'Guys and Dolls' Delights London." *New York Post* 19 July 1953.
_____. "The Lively World of Damon Runyon." *New York Post* 26 Nov. 1950.

Wolf, Matt. "American Musicals, as Tailored by the British." *New York Times*, 28 Aug. 1994, H5.

Woolcott, Alexander. "The Deep, Tangled Kaufman." *New Yorker* 18 May 1929, 26-29.

**AGMV** Marquis

MEMBER OF SCABRINI MEDIA

Quebec, Canada
2002